The Confederate Homefront

—— THE ——
CONFEDERATE HOMEFRONT

A History in Documents

WALLACE HETTLE

LOUISIANA STATE UNIVERSITY PRESS

BATON ROUGE

Published by Louisiana State University Press
Copyright © 2017 by Louisiana State University Press
All rights reserved
Manufactured in the United States of America
First printing

Designer: Barbara Neely Bourgoyne
Typeface: Ingeborg
Printer and binder: McNaughton & Gunn, Inc.

Library of Congress Cataloging-in-Publication Data

Names: Hettle, Wallace, 1962– compiler.
Title: The Confederate homefront : a history in documents / Wallace Hettle.
Description: Baton Rouge : Louisiana State University Press, [2017] | Includes index.
Identifiers: LCCN 2016041481| ISBN 978-0-8071-6755-7 (cloth: alk. paper) |
    ISBN 978-0-8071-6572-0 (pbk. : alk. paper) | ISBN 978-0-8071-6573-7 (pdf) |
    ISBN 978-0-8071-6574-4 (epub) | ISBN 978-0-8071-6575-1 (mobi)
Subjects: LCSH: Confederate States of America—History—Sources. | United States—
    History—Civil War, 1861–1865—Sources.
Classification: LCC E487 .H58 2017 | DDC 973.7/13—dc23
LC record available at https://lccn.loc.gov/2016041481

For Arlo

CONTENTS

PREFACE xi

———— 1861 ————

1. "Utter Subjugation Awaits Us in the Union": Mississippi
   Secedes 3
2. A Slave Reacts to the Election of Lincoln 6
3. Slavery: The Cornerstone of the Confederacy 10
4. Charleston and the First Shot of the War 13
5. Fear of a Slave Rebellion in Mississippi (Two Documents) 16
6. A Slave's View of Religion, Emancipation, and Abraham Lincoln 20
7. The Union Reacts to Runaway Slaves (Two Documents) 22
8. A Newspaper Editor Reluctantly Supports Secession 26
9. A North Carolina Minister Endorses the War 29
10. A Southern Woman Embraces the Confederate Cause 32
11. Mark Twain's "Campaign That Failed" 35
12. A Slave Debates Politics with Her Owners 40
13. A White Family Weighs the Consequences of War 42
14. South Carolina Planters Abandon the Coastline 45

———— 1862 ————

15. "Prayers for Freedom": An Ex-Slave Remembers the War 49
16. Conscription and the Confederacy: A View from South
    Carolina 51
17. A Louisiana Family Flees from the Union Army 53
18. The Prison Diary of a Tennessee Unionist 56

19. The Governor of Georgia Denounces the Draft 59
20. The Union's Attack on Richmond in 1862: A View from within the City 61
21. The Arrest of a Virginia Dissenter 64
22. A Black Abolitionist on Teaching Former Slaves 66
23. Andrew Johnson and Political Conflict in Tennessee (Two Documents) 69
24. Remembering the Death of a Confederate Soldier 73
25. Domestic Slavery and the Confederate Cause 76
26. The Amazing Escape of Robert Smalls, a Slave and Steamboat Pilot 79
27. Confederate Women and Union Troops in Occupied New Orleans 84
28. A Slave's "Faithfulness and Devotion" 86
29. Union Occupation and Plantation Labor in the Mississippi Valley 88

—— 1863 ——

30. A Civilian on the Death of a Soldier 93
31. Anti-Semitism in the Confederacy 96
32. A Bread Riot in Richmond (Four Documents) 99
33. A Louisiana Woman Describes the Arrival of Union Troops 106
34. The Confederate Public Mourns a Hero 111
35. The Mysterious Death of a Slave Woman 113
36. Runaway Slave Advertisements 116
37. A Confederate Partisan on the Aftermath of Battle 119
38. A Confederate Governor on the War at Home 121
39. An Alabama "Belle" Leaves Home 124
40. Masters and Slaves in Occupied Mississippi 126
41. A Political Prisoner Writes to Abraham Lincoln 128
42. Union Soldiers Loot Jefferson Davis's Possessions 131
43. A Former Soldier Begins to Farm (Three Documents) 135
44. A Prisoner of War Encounters Southern Women 140
45. The Confederate War Department and the Impressment of Slaves 142

46. William T. Sherman and Hard War 145
47. A Refugee Bemoans the Brutality of the War 147

—— 1864 ——

48. A Southern Woman's Despair 151
49. Confederate Emancipation: A Proposal 153
50. "This Is Our Country": A Meeting of Former Slaves 157
51. "You Got My Hog!": A Theft by Confederate Soldiers 159
52. Jefferson Davis's Fugitive Slave 163
53. A Former Slave Describes a Death in His Master's Family 165
54. A Southern Publisher on the Consequences of Surrender 167
55. An Editorial Praises the Restraint of Black Soldiers 169
56. The Transition from Slavery to Free Labor in the Mississippi Valley 171
57. A Former Mississippi Slave Describes a Failed Escape Attempt 173
58. Jefferson Davis Addresses the Public 178

—— 1865 ——

59. A Texas Newspaper Lacks News 183
60. Confederate Emancipation (Three Documents) 185
61. A South Carolina Writer Describes the Burning of Columbia 191
62. A Former Slave Remembers Emancipation 194
63. A White Officer Describes Freedmen Who Fought in the Union Army 197
64. "How Freedom Came" 199
65. Booker T. Washington Recalls Slavery and Freedom 202
66. "My Unmitigated Hatred to Yankee Rule": Edmund Ruffin's Suicide 206

ACKNOWLEDGMENTS 209
INDEX 211

PREFACE

The Civil War began with a bang. On the morning of April 12, 1861, Edmund Ruffin, an elderly civilian from Virginia, fired the first shot of the rebellion. Ruffin was famous as a proslavery extremist who had long agitated for the South to leave the Union. Highly committed to southern independence, he had rushed to South Carolina after seven Deep South states left the Union in January 1861. In tribute to his political contribution, and despite his age, Ruffin had been asked to join a militia in Charleston as an artilleryman. In that capacity, he fired the first shot of the war at Fort Sumter, a federal installation in Charleston's harbor. While others later claimed to have fired first, Ruffin declared, "Of course I was highly gratified at the compliment, & delighted to perform the service—which I did."[1] Following Ruffin, scores of cannon immediately opened fire.

For many, the American Civil War conjures up visions of soldiers on rural battlefields, such as Antietam and Gettysburg. Yet the first salvo was unleashed by a civilian in Charleston, the largest city in South Carolina. The war began there for good reason: South Carolina was the first state to secede from the Union, and Charleston became known as the "Cradle of the Confederacy." If the rebels could not defend themselves in Charleston, they not could survive. So the firing began, and the war came. The Union commander at Fort Sumter, the southern-born Major Robert Anderson, found himself outgunned and low on provisions. He had little choice but to capitulate.

In some accounts, the war ended when Robert E. Lee's army

---

1. William Scarborough, ed., *The Diary of Edmund Ruffin,* vol. 1, *Toward Independence, October 1856–April 1861* (Baton Rouge: Louisiana State Univ. Press), 588.

surrendered at the Appomattox Court House in Virginia on April 9, 1865. But for the elderly Ruffin, the Confederacy ended with another bang. On June 18, 1865, Ruffin loaded a musket, put it in his mouth, and pulled the trigger. It misfired. Hearing the gun's report, his family came running to save him. Before they could intervene, Ruffin reloaded and killed himself. In his suicide note, he detailed his fear that Supreme Court Chief Justice Salmon P. Chase was "planting the seeds of future civil war between . . . the blacks & whites." He condemned the "Yankees" for their "robbery, rapine & destruction, & house-burning, all committed contrary to the laws of war on non-combatant residents, & still worse on aged men & helpless women!"[2] While he bemoaned the plight of noncombatants, Ruffin had delayed his suicide for two months. He had held out hope that Confederates in Texas, isolated from the rest of the South by the Union-controlled Mississippi River, could continue to fight.[3]

Slaves in Texas were among the last to learn of the Union's victory. Federal soldiers arrived there on June 19, 1865, effectively ending human bondage in that state. African American communities across the country celebrate that day as a holiday, "Juneteenth." For descendants of slaves, Juneteenth marks a hard-won victory for freedom. Americans, black and white, should remember Juneteenth, as it commemorates American hopes to achieve liberty for all. Emancipation was the greatest achievement of the Civil War era, but the defense of liberty and equality raised on Juneteenth remain to be finished.

Ironically, Ruffin, living in the distant state of Virginia, killed himself just the day before emancipation in Texas. The radical secessionist began the war triumphantly, and ended it in despair. He ended the war just as he had begun it: by firing a gun. Today he is largely forgotten, and perhaps that is for the best. He leaves a legacy of hatred that we should put in the past. With hope for the future, we should remember Juneteenth.

---

2. Ibid., 3:945–46, 924.
3. Ibid., 3:945.

This book offers representative documents about people on the Confederate home front during the Civil War. However, in collecting and organizing these documents, I found that a rigid distinction between "home" and the "battlefield" obscures the complexity of the war years. Because the Civil War was fought almost entirely in the South, the experiences of southerners, black and white, were intertwined with the actions of soldiers on both sides of the conflict. While this book contains no documents regarding military tactics, it does depict the way that military events and ideas contributed to civilian experiences.

The key actors in this collection are a diverse group. They include slaves, ministers, and newspaper editors who sought to explain or oppose the conflict. Other documents explore how the relatives of soldiers responded to the deaths of heroes and loved ones. The plight of civilian refugees and the destruction caused by guerrillas, expressed in several of these documents, can be used as a lens to view similar displacements in our times.

To understand the central role of slavery in the conflict, this collection includes a variety of sources, including orders and reports from soldiers. For example, as slaves began to emancipate themselves by running away from their masters, many sought the protection of the Union military. Runaway slaves forced the Union military to debate their status, and these changing policies helped determine the war's outcome. Their labor in camps and fighting as soldiers helped bring the Union to victory. Confederate armies also shaped the experience of civilians when they took goods, including food and slaves, from them in a haphazard and arbitrary manner. When rank-and-file soldiers strayed outside of camp, the need for food sometimes drove them to outright theft. Civilians constantly followed the reporting of military actions, fearing for their loved ones in the ranks or the possibility of Union soldiers arriving at their homes. Ordinary people, including women and children, fled as Union armies advanced.

In peacetime, tradition may hold sway. But when change comes, as it did in the Confederacy, it can happen with astonishing intensity. Southerners, who knew they lived in uncommon times, recorded their stories as never before. They generated an extraordinary array of documents, including letters, diaries, newspapers, speeches, sermons, and novels. After the war ended, the outpouring of words continued in the form of memoirs, autobiographies, and recorded interviews.

Historians seek out evidence, interpret its significance, and attempt to persuade others to share their point of view. Primary sources, such as the documents included in this book, are the building blocks of historical teaching, writing, and learning, as historians use them to shape stories and interpretations of the past. Written documents may originate in any time or place, whether it is medieval England or nineteenth-century America. Significant historical sources do not have to be words recorded on paper—some historians also draw on physical objects, from teapots to fashionable clothing. But for most Civil War historians, words from the past are essential.

At first glance, finding and selecting a few dozen documents on the Confederacy sounds like an easy task. By some estimates, historians had produced fifty thousand books on the conflict by the 1960s. (After that, weary bibliographers stopped counting.) Ironically, the enormous number of documents made the task more difficult. It required finding a few needles in the most enormous haystack one could imagine. However, a key theme soon emerged. In the memoirs and diaries of elite women, in the words of white male civilians, both loyal and disloyal to the cause, in the abundant newspaper records, slavery again and again jumped to the forefront. This book does not address the longstanding debate about whether slavery caused the Civil War. Instead, the documents compiled here suggest that once the war began, it brought the system of slavery to center stage. Southerners lived in a society that was socially, economically, and culturally based on human bondage. Slavery had begun to unravel long before Lincoln's Emancipation Proclamation took effect. Those who lived through the experience could scarcely have avoided the subject.

Nineteenth-century Americans, confronted with the greatest crisis in our nation's history, wrote extraordinarily provocative and eloquent prose. These people exemplified both the best and worst in human nature. Their words are sometimes disconcerting or even shameful, but at the same time many are inspiring, puzzling, or fascinating. These documents make it possible for the reader to do what historians do: to think about the past critically and creatively, to produce one's own interpretation of distant events.

In introducing and choosing documents, I have tried to be conscious of rapid changes in our culture of reading. Today's reading habits have, in large part, been shaped by the Internet, especially social media and texting—on Twitter, the maximum number of characters for each tweet is 140. Many, including some young people, have bemoaned the relative curtness of our culture. But Lincoln's Gettysburg Address, the most eloquent speech of the nineteenth century, contained only 272 words. In selecting and commenting on the relatively brief documents and excerpts here, I have tried to remember William Shakespeare's admonition that "brevity is the soul of wit."

Sometimes a phrase becomes a cliché because it is true, and no historical verity is more certain than the idea that every generation writes its own history. For decades after the war, most studies of the Confederacy focused on military and political topics. A traditional account of a heroic southern "Lost Cause" dominated the literature. In this interpretation, brilliant leaders, such as Robert E. Lee, "Stonewall" Jackson, and Jeb Stuart fought valiantly and were defeated only because the Union's greater population and economic resources triumphed over Confederate heroism. Further, southern enthusiasm to defend their independence trumped Union incompetence for four years. In the first half of the twentieth century, the notable Virginia-based Civil War historian Douglas Southall Freeman used evocative prose to buttress his exalted view of Robert E. Lee. In Freeman's opinion, Lee exemplified the virtues of a white southern "race." More recently, the novelist and historian Shelby Foote has offered a highly sympathetic view of the Confederate military in his trilogy on the war.

By the fiftieth anniversary of the war, statues of Robert E. Lee, "Stonewall" Jackson, and Jefferson Davis dotted the southern landscape. Epic films such as *The Birth of a Nation* (1915) and *Gone with the Wind* (1939) paid tribute to white southerners, both men and women, who were portrayed as steadfast supporters of the cause. This outdated perspective portrayed slaves as watching passively, or even supporting their masters' war.

During the last several decades, Civil War historians have rejected hero worship and moved "beyond the battlefield." In large part, altered views of the conflict reflect broader changes in society and the historical profession. Until the 1960s, white men so dominated the most prestigious history departments that many entry-level positions were not even publicly advertised. However, by the 1960s, first-generation college students, including African Americans and women, joined the profession. Many of these scholars painted a more inclusive picture of southern life during the war, focusing on ordinary people, creating a new framework for viewing the past. Historians examined previously neglected groups, a scholarly movement often described as a "new social history" or "history from below." These historians provided a more inclusive understanding of the Civil War era.

James McPherson's book *Battle Cry of Freedom,* published in 1988, remains highly influential today, and for good reason. It represented the culmination of scholarship by the generation of historians who lived through the successes of the civil rights movement. These scholars correctly hailed emancipation as a triumph and argued, contrary to earlier writers, that the war's results justified its terrible human price. In addition, there were cultural landmarks, such as the film *Glory* (1989) and Ken Burns's massive PBS documentary *The Civil War* (1990).

Martin Luther King Jr. famously said that the arc of history bends toward justice. It is hard to dispute the words of a hero, but many today are less optimistic about achieving justice than the previous generation of baby boomers. Yet, paradoxically, our recent past may well be remembered for doing something that was once unthinkable: electing an African American president twice. In 2008, Barack Obama's success sparked optimistic discussions of America as a new "post-racial" society. For scholars like me, who came of age in an era of limits, economic inequality, and continuing racial bias, this optimistic view seems hopelessly naive.

Further, failed wars in Afghanistan and Iraq have resulted in increased skepticism about war advancing the social good. Indeed, a growing number of scholars have urged Civil War historians to revise our thinking about the war. Calls to discard the triumphant views epitomized by *Glory* and to fully portray the human tragedy of the war are gaining a broader hearing. One thing is certain: as society changes, historical insight of the war will change with it. In recent cultural history, depictions of the war era have varied widely. The superb film *Twelve Years a Slave* (2013) brought a realistic picture of slavery, based on the experiences of a former slave, before a mass audience. Unfortunately, the recent film *Django Unchained* (2012) by acclaimed director Quentin Tarantino exploited the history of slavery, using it as a pretense for mindless violence. In our present context, the Confederate experience remains open to misinterpretation.

Even today, no political symbol evokes more controversy than the Confederate battle flag, known by some as the "Stars and Bars." Those who wish to fly the flag claim they want to preserve southern "heritage." But the custom of flying that flag on government buildings is a recent invention. Some southern politicians began to raise the banner in the 1960s as a protest against the civil rights movement. Entire books have examined the flag's history, and bloggers rehash the arguments about it on a daily basis. The persistent display is dispiriting, and not only because it exemplifies a misuse of history. It also serves as a symbol for racially polarized views over present-day issues, such as affirmative action and minority voting rights. Hopefully, the documents here will help readers shape their own views on such debates in our present society and culture.

The people of the Civil War South resemble us—whites and blacks, men and women, soldiers and civilians. They sought security and they risked their lives for freedom. Many of them acted selflessly, others committed atrocities. Some struggled for local control of the war effort, while others saw a need for centralized authority. They do not leave us with a single heritage of the Civil War South, but rather with multiple perspectives on a world that was changing even more rapidly than our own. When politicians honor the heritage of another time and place, it usually is an empty gesture. Historians can do better. We can approach these documents with a spirit of humility, acknowledging that our understanding of their world can never be complete.

History is about people, and most of us are complicated enough to defy easy categorization into themes or subject areas. I have therefore arranged the documents in rough chronological order. However, some compelling sources, especially slave narratives and oral histories, are difficult to pin down with precise dates. Their placements are based on my educated guesses regarding the approximate time of the events they depict.

In almost all instances, I have preserved the spelling and phrasing of the original documents. In a few cases I have made silent corrections rather than use the patronizing term [*sic*]. In some passages I have added my own words within brackets for the sake of clarity or to establish historical context or add details, such as the full names of prominent figures. This book includes interviews with ex-slaves conducted by the Works Progress Administration (WPA) in the 1930s. Interviewers usually transcribed these documents in a racially stereotyped and patronizing black dialect. I have altered the original interview transcripts by rendering them in standard English, a change that increases clarity and treats the former slaves with respect.

1861

"UTTER SUBJUGATION AWAITS US IN THE UNION": MISSISSIPPI SECEDES

In the "secession winter" of 1860–61, politicians from the Deep South— South Carolina, Alabama, Georgia, Texas, Florida, Louisiana, and Mississippi—engineered the exit of their states from the Union. In this "Declaration," written while the so-called Border States of the Upper South continued to debate the wisdom of secession, Mississippi's political leaders frankly noted that slavery was the cause of disunion.

In the momentous step which our State has taken of dissolving its connection with the government of which we so long formed a part, it is but just that we should declare the prominent reasons which have induced our course.

Our position is thoroughly identified with the institution of slavery—the greatest material interest of the world. Its labor supplies the product which constitutes by far the largest and most important portions of the commerce of the earth. These products are peculiar to the climate verging on the tropical regions, and by an impervious law of nature none but the black race can bear exposure to the tropical sun. These products have become necessities of the world, and a blow at slavery is a blow at commerce and civilization. That blow has been long aimed at the institution, and was at the point of reaching its consummation. There was no choice left us but submission to the mandates of abolition, or a dissolution of the Union, whose principles had been subverted to work out our ruin.

That we do not overstate the dangers to our institution, a reference to a few facts will sufficiently prove.

The hostility to this institution commenced before the adoption of the Constitution, and was manifested in the well-known Ordinance of 1787, in regard to the Northwestern Territory.

The feeling increased, until, in 1819–20, it deprived the South of more than half the vast territory acquired from France.

The same hostility dismembered Texas and seized upon all the territory acquired from Mexico.

It has grown until it denies the right of property in slaves, and refuses protection to that right on the high seas, in the Territories, and wherever the government of the United States has jurisdiction.

It refuses the admission of new slave States into the Union, and seeks to extinguish it by confining it with in its present limits, denying the power of expansion.

It tramples the original equality of the South underfoot.

It has nullified the Fugitive Slave Law in almost every free State in the Union, and has utterly broken the compact which our fathers pledged their faith to maintain.

It advocates negro equality, socially and politically, and promotes insurrection and incendiarism in our midst.

It has enlisted its press, its pulpit and its schools against us, until the whole popular mind of the North is excited and inflamed with prejudice.

It has made combinations and formed associations to carry out its schemes of emancipation in the States and wherever else slavery exists.

It seeks not to elevate or to support the slave, but to destroy his present condition without providing a better.

It has invaded a State, and invested with the honors of martyrdom the wretch whose purpose was to apply flames to our dwellings, and the weapons of destruction to our lives.

It has broken every compact into which it has entered for our security.

It has given indubitable evidence of its design to ruin our agriculture, to prostrate our industrial pursuits and to destroy our social system.

It knows no relenting or hesitation in its purposes; it stops not in its march of aggression, and leaves us no room to hope for cessation or for pause.

It has recently obtained control of the Government, by the prosecution of its unhallowed schemes, and destroyed the last expectation of living together in friendship and brotherhood.

Utter subjugation awaits us in the Union, if we should consent longer to remain in it. It is not a matter of choice, but of necessity. We must either submit to degradation, and to the loss of property worth four billions of money, or we must secede from the Union framed by our fathers, to secure this as well as every other species of property. For far less cause than this, our fathers separated from the Crown of England.

Our decision is made. We follow their footsteps. We embrace the alternative of separation; and for the reasons here stated, we resolve to maintain our rights with the full consciousness of the justice of our course, and the undoubting belief of our ability to maintain it.

Mississippi Secession Convention, "A Declaration of the Immediate Causes Which Induce and Justify the Secession of Mississippi from the Federal Union and the Ordinance of Secession, January 26, 1861," in *Commemoration of the Centennial of the Civil War* (Jackson: Mississippi Commission on the War Between the States, 1962), appendix 3.

2

A SLAVE REACTS TO THE ELECTION
OF LINCOLN

*William Webb, who learned to read during the war, left a harrowing
account of his escape to freedom. After the conflict ended, publishers
lost interest in slave narratives, and his short book, published with
an obscure midwestern press, received little attention. The work is
less polished than the best narratives written before the war, such
as those of Frederick Douglass, Solomon Northup, or Harriet Jacobs.
However, this former slave's understated observations of secession
and the Civil War are consistent with depictions of slavery from other
sources. The "big business" he mentions refers to fomenting agitation
among fellow slaves.*

About seven months before the election of Lincoln, my main master sold me. He said the next President that was elected, would be
an Abolitionist, and he thought the colored people would be set free,
and that he would sell me, and put the money in his pocket. He sold
me for fifteen hundred dollars cash, but I was doing such big business that I did not mind it at all. I was not much pleased with the
man that bought me. At that time I was receiving news from a great
many States. I astonished the man that bought me, by telling him
how things were going on in different States, till he thought I must
be a wizard, or something worse. Time passed off very well with me.
I had all the business I was able to attend to. After the nomination,
we could hear nothing in Kentucky, but the names of [John] Bell
and [Stephen] Douglas. There was nothing heard about Lincoln till a
while before the election came off. The name of Lincoln going to free
the slaves, was the next news heard by the colored people, and the

blessed news flew from one State to another, and the colored people
all over the State knew who was their friend, and we understood the
whole matter. Then my friend sent me word that they were getting up
soldiers in Mississippi and at other points fixing for war. Then I sent
news for everybody to pray that Lincoln would be elected. The time
passed away, and the election came off. Lincoln was elected and great
thanks went up to the Lord from the colored people. The next news
we heard, was a great talk about war. That kept growing stronger and
stronger in the land, till we saw that we had to do something else. We
sent out word all over, in all the States, for the colored people not to
take up arms for the slaveholders. Everything was well understood
among the colored people. My friends sent me word from Mississippi,
that they were up in arms. There was great joy among the slaves. I
was made a spy for the Rebels, but I wanted that position to gain
my other points. I left with a good understanding with my leaders.
I stayed with the rebels long enough. I had learned all I wanted to
know, and I knew they did not wish me much good will. The next
fight that took place was at Belmont, below Cairo. The Republicans
got beat down there. I wept bitter tears. I thought then I had better
leave. The Yankee soldiers landed at Paducah, Kentucky. I went down
to see them once in a while. My master thought I was going to run
away and stay with the Yankee soldiers. A crowd of the slaveholders
came and bound me with ropes and carried me to the blacksmith
shop, and put a shackle around my ankle and a six foot chain fastened
to it, and he took me to a speculator nine miles from Mayfield. Those
men that carried me to the speculator, told him to keep me bound
tight, for I was a dangerous man, and if he did not mind, I would get
away from him. We got there on Sunday evening. The speculator put
me up-stairs in his house, and what he was going to do with me, I am
not able to say. That night a voice spoke to me, saying, "be of good
cheer, I will be along with you." When the morning came, it come to
my mind what I must do. I went down to breakfast and I said to the
old colored woman, who looked as if she was seventy years old, to
give me a small file. She got a file and handed it to me and I slipped
it into my pocket. She said, you are that man I have heard so much
about, and I know you will not betray me. I told her that I would

never betray her in the world. Then I called the speculator and told him I wanted to go up-stairs again. He carried me up-stairs, and I told him I would like some rags to wrap around that shackle, it was hurting my ankle. He gave me some rags, and I wrapped them around the shackle and some of the links. I did that in order to file the chain off, and if he came up, I could wrap the rags around and he would not notice it. I filed the chain, and got through about two hours before sunset, and when the chain parted, it appeared to me as if it opened an inch wide. I tied a rotten string around the chain, so that I could break it easy, and I wrapped the rags around it the same as I had them. I looked out of the window and marked out my way to escape, when night came on. When night came, he carried me down to supper. After he carried me down, I told him I wanted to go out in the yard. It was dark, and when the speculator took me out in the yard I broke the chain and escaped. I had twenty-seven miles to go to Paducah, Kentucky, to get to the Union soldiers. The next morning by sunrise, I was in Paducah. When I got there, I went to General Wallace and Captain Lyman, and they asked me if I could cook. I said yes. I still had the iron shackle on my leg. They carried me down to the blacksmith's and had the shackle filed off. Captain Lyman told me he thought I was very ambitious to file that chain and escape. He said he would keep me as long as I would stay with him. They gave me the keys of every thing around the house. I was well pleased; but they were taking the slaves back, and I was afraid they would arrest me and carry me back, but Captain Lyman promised me, that they should never get me. In about three days my master came there after me. General Wallace had a guard around his house, and he had to go through the guard before he could get to General Wallace. The guard told General Wallace that a gentleman wanted to speak to him. The General told him to come in. When he came in, the General asked him his business. He said, you have a boy in here I want. The General questioned him very close. The General asked him what I had done to have such iron shackles on my leg. He told him I had not done anything. General Wallace told him he guessed he would keep me, and told him never to come back after me any more, for if he did he would arrest him. Then I had a good time. I enjoyed myself better than I had ever done before in my life. I sent out word to different points, that I was at the headquarters of the Abolitionists. I told them that Fremont was in Missouri, freeing all the colored people. They sent back a message enjoying the good news, and wishing me much enjoyment that I was free. General Wallace said he was looking for his wife, and when she went back home, I could go with her. He told me I must be a good fellow, and learn to read, for his wife would let me go to school, and I must take care of things around the house. His wife came. He told her about my going home with her, and she was much pleased to have me go with her. Soon after, the order came for us to march around Mayfield in the direction of Fort Henry.

William Webb, *The History of William Webb, Composed by Himself* (Detroit: Egbert Hoekstra, Printer, 1873), 30–35.

3

SLAVERY: THE CORNERSTONE OF
THE CONFEDERACY

Serving in the House of Representatives in the 1840s, Abraham Lincoln and a fellow Whig Party member, Alexander Stephens of Georgia, became friends. After Lincoln's election in November 1860, Stephens initially opposed secession. He argued that it would bring a war that could jeopardize slavery's existence and the region's prosperity. After Georgia left the Union on January 2, 1861, Stephens embraced the Confederate cause. Newly inaugurated as the vice president of the Confederacy, Stephens gave this address, often called the "Cornerstone" speech, which illustrated the rapid transformation of his political views.

This new constitution, or form of government, constitutes the subject to which your attention will be partly invited. In reference to it, I make this first general remark: it amply secures all our ancient rights, franchises, and liberties. All of the great principles of Magna Charta are retained in it. No person is deprived of life, liberty, or property, but by the judgment of his peers under the laws of the land. The great principle of religious liberty, which was the honor and pride of the old Constitution, is still maintained and secured. All the essentials of this old Constitution, which have endeared it to the hearts of the American people, have been preserved and perpetuated. . . .

But not to be tedious in enumerating the numerous changes for the better, allow me to allude to one other though last, not least: the new Constitution has put to rest *forever* all the agitating questions relating to our peculiar institution—African slavery as it exists among us—the proper *status* of the negro in our form of civilization. This was the immediate cause of the late rupture and present revolution.

Jefferson, in his forecast, had anticipated this, as the "rock upon which the old Union would split." He was right. What was conjecture with him is now a realized fact. But whether he fully comprehended the great truth upon which that rock *stood* and *stands,* may be doubted. The prevailing ideas entertained by him and most of the leading statesmen at the time of the formation of the old Constitution were, that the enslavement of the African was in violation of the laws of nature; that it was wrong in *principle,* socially, morally and politically. It was an evil they knew not well how to deal with; but the general opinion of the men of that day was that, somehow or other, in the order of Providence, the institution would be evanescent and pass away. This idea, though not incorporated in the Constitution, was the prevailing idea at the time. The Constitution, it is true, secured every essential guarantee of the institution while it should last, and hence no argument can be justly used against the constitutional guarantees thus secured, because of the common sentiment of the day. Those ideas, however, were fundamentally wrong. They rested upon the assumption of the equality of races. This was an error. It was a sandy foundation, and the idea of a Government built upon it—when the "storm came and wind blew, it *fell.*"

Our new Government is founded upon exactly the opposite idea; its foundations are laid, its cornerstone rests, upon the great truth that the negro is not equal to the white man; that slavery—subordination to the superior race—is his natural and moral condition. (Applause.)

This, our new Government, is the first, in the history of the world, based upon this great physical, philosophical, and moral truth. This truth has been slow in the process of its development, like all other truths in the various departments of science. It is so even amongst us. Many who hear me, perhaps, can recollect well that this truth was not generally admitted, even within their day. The errors of the past generation still clung to many as late as twenty years ago. Those at the North who still cling to these errors with a zeal above knowledge, we justly denominate fanatics. All fanaticism springs from an aberration of the mind—from a defect in reasoning. It is a species of insanity. One of the most striking characteristics of insanity, in many instances, is forming correct conclusions from fancied or erroneous premises; so with the anti-slavery fanatics; their conclusions are right if their premises are. They assume that the negro is equal, and hence conclude that he is entitled to equal privileges and rights with the white man. If their premises were correct, their conclusions would be logical and just; but their premises being wrong, their whole argument fails. I recollect once of having heard a gentleman from one of the Northern States, of great power and ability, announce in the House of Representatives, with imposing effect, that we of the South would be compelled, ultimately, to yield upon the subject of slavery; that it was as impossible to war successfully against a principle in politics, as it was in physics or mechanics. That the principle would ultimately prevail. That we, in maintaining slavery as it exists with us, were warring against a principle, a principle founded in nature, the principle of the equality of man. The reply I made to him was, that upon his own grounds we should succeed, and that he and his associates in their crusade against our institutions would ultimately fail. The truth announced, that it was impossible to war successfully against a principle in politics as well as in physics and mechanics, I admitted, but told him it was he and those acting with him who were warring against a principle. They were attempting to make things equal which the Creator had made unequal.

"A Speech by Hon. Alexander H. Stephens, Vice President of the Confederate States of America, Delivered at the Atheneum, Savannah [Georgia], March 22, 1861," in Edward A. Pollard, *Echoes from the South* (New York: E. B. Treat, 1866), 84–87.

——— 4 ———

CHARLESTON AND THE FIRST SHOT
OF THE WAR

*In the 1850s, Edmund Ruffin, a native of Virginia, became famous
as an extremist campaigner for secession, or, as they were otherwise
known, a "fire-eater." In reward for his political advocacy, a South
Carolina militia company asked him to fire the first shot of the war.
Ruffin's opening salvo began a massive artillery barrage that forced the
surrender of Fort Sumter, a federal installation in the harbor just off
Charleston, South Carolina. While other southern men later claimed
the dubious honor of firing the first shot, Ruffin's account of events is
based on good contemporary evidence.*

*Since the majority of South Carolina residents were slaves and
South Carolina was the first state to secede from the Union, it was
fitting that the first battle took place in Charleston. The fact that the
fighting began in a city also demonstrated that in this war there would
be no clear line between the home front and the battlefield.*

April 12.

Before 4 a.m. the drums beat for parade & our company was speedily on the march to the batteries which they were to man. At 4:30,
a signal shell was thrown from a mortar battery at Fort Johnson,
which had been before ordered to be taken as the command for
immediate attack—& the firing from all the batteries bearing on
Fort Sumter next began in the order arranged—which was that the
discharges should be two minutes apart, & the round of all the pieces
& batteries to be completed in 32 minutes, & then to begin again.
The night before, when expecting to engage, Captain Cuthbert had
notified me that his company requested of me to discharge the first

cannon to be fired, which was their 64 lb. Columbiad, loaded with shell. By order of Gen. Beauregard, made known on the afternoon of the 11th, the attack was to be commenced by the first shot at the fort being fired by the Palmetto Guard, & from the Iron Battery. In accepting and acting upon this highly appreciated compliment, that company made me its instrument. [O]f course I was highly gratified by the compliment, & delighted to perform the service—which I did. The shell struck the fort, at the north-east angle of the parapet. The firing then proceeded, as stated from 14 different batteries, including Fort Moultrie & the floating battery, which had been placed for this purpose in the cove, back of Sullivan's Island. Most of both shot & shells, at first, missed the fort. But many struck, & the proportion of balls & shells increased with practice. To all this firing, not a gun was fired in return, for two hours or more—& I was fearful that Major Anderson, relying on the security of his men in the covered casemates, proof against shells, & in the strength of the walls against breaching by balls—& in the impossibility of successful storming of the strong fortress, surrounded by water, did not intend to fire at all. It would have cheapened our conquest of the fort, if effected, if no hostile defence had been made—& still more increased the disgrace of failure. So it was gratifying to all of us when Major Anderson opened his fire.

For Ruffin, a radical who had spent years in political isolation, the battle for Fort Sumter felt like personal vindication.

April 15.

Since my first coming to S.C. in last November, I have been received & treated by all persons with whom I have come in contact, with great kindness & attention, as I was really a public benefactor of rare merit. From entire strangers, & in many cases persons of humble position as well as the higher classes, in numerous cases I have received manifestations of great respect & higher appreciation. But since the beginning of my recent military service, & still more since the surrender of Fort Sumter, the evidences of general popular favor & expressions of individual consideration & applause have increased ten-fold, & make me the object of such great distinction.

William Augusta Kauffman Scarborough, ed., *The Diary of Edmund Ruffin,* vol. 1, *Toward Independence, October 1856–April 1861* (Baton Rouge: Louisiana State Univ. Press, 1972), 588–89, 602.

FEAR OF A SLAVE REBELLION IN MISSISSIPPI
(TWO DOCUMENTS)

In the rich cotton lands of the Mississippi River delta, where slaves outnumbered whites, slaveholders worried that the election of Lincoln might spark rebellion. In 1861, suspicious whites in Adams County, Mississippi, who feared that rebellion was imminent, executed at least forty slaves to stave off a dreaded uprising. No record of these events appeared in newspapers because leaders believed that word of the alleged conspiracy would encourage more such plots. Local whites so closely held news of the case that it dropped out of historical memory for more than a century, until it was rediscovered through historical research published in the 1990s.

Gov' J J Pettus

Dear Sir

On my return from Jackson I found the greatest state of excitement caused by the discovery—of an organization by the negros for the purpos of riseing on the 4th of July next at which time [they] had been induced to believe Lincons troops would be here for the purpos of freeing them all. This was discovered by Mr Isaac Harrison of Tensas parrish La which lies oposite Jefferson County. Mr David Harrison, brother to the former, had sent his children on a visit to their uncle. Being aware that the negros all knew of the war and what it was for, Mr Isaac Harrison secreted himself under the house and heared the conversation between his boy and his brothers. The perport of which was about this. That when Lincons came down each one was to kill his master and that they would later the fine houses and the white women. Mr Isaac Harrison's boy has paid the penalty. The other is still in durance vile and has disclosed their plan and on the day I left Jackson on Saturday two negros one belonging to Mr Darden (who was captain) the other the property of Mr Prosper K. Montgomery 1st Lieutenant were hung by the Gentlemen of the neighbourhood. There are 5 white men and 2 negros now in jail suspected of being in the plot. And the citizens are still investigating the matter with the view of bring all criminals to sumary justice. In consequence of this state of affairs I learn from Captain W L Harper the citizens of Jefferson are not willing any more companys should leave the county. I told him that I considered we were in honor bound to go and he has consented to go to New Orleans at Co'ln French's suggestion and take two or three men with them to learn the drill[.] Now Sir it is with you to say whether we shall go under the circumstances or not[.] We are anxious to do so. Whether we will now get that aid from the citizens we had assurances of previously I am unable to say as I have not been home long enough to ascertain their sentiments. We have now about half horses sufficient for the battery and I am well assured we can get men enough[.] After this would it not be adviseable to keep as many of the companys in the river countys at home as possible where thelargest negro population is. As for myself I dont apprehend that Lincons forces will ever reach here[.] Still there are many who live in great fear[.] I am a ware there are many in the *cow* countys who are anxious and willing to go if they could be assured their familys could or would be provided for. I am told some of the wealthiest planters in Adams are going to Europe (I presume for safty.) If such be the fact and they do not subscribe in proportion to their means to protect their property, I hope their property will be confiscated and sold to support those and the familys of those who have little or no interest in the county. Govr Moon of La I am informed has expressly forbiden any more troops from the river parishes leaving and has said if necessary would charter a Steam Boat and put troops on her so that he could send them to any parish on the river where there was an out-break.

You will please share this to Coln S. G. French. I will advise him when to ship the two guns[.] I should not under other circumstances obtruded myself on your time and patience[.]
accept for yourself—my highest regards &c
your friend, *How Hines*

How[ell] Hines to Gov. J. J. Pettus, May 14, 1861, in Governors Papers, Mississippi Department of Archives and History.

Jo. D. L. Davenport to Governor
Gov Pettus
Jackson Mi

Dear Sir:
. . . A plot has been discovered and [alrea]dy three Negroes have gone the way of all flesh or rather paid the penalty by the forfeiture of their lives. We have at this time five white men and one negro in our jail who will doubtless pull hemp. There are others who we have not yet succeeded in arresting. In a population of 650 voters surrounded by 11,000 slaves with one company already in the field, of over one hundred men "Charley Clark Rifles" and three other companies mustered into the service awaiting your call. Has set me to thinking where I could be of the most service to my Country, *at home* or *in the army.* You will see that nothing but eternal Vigilance will keep down the enemy at home as well as on our frontier and costs [coasts?]. The plans as developed are of the most diabolical character, the white males were all to be destroyed—such of the females as suited their fancy were to be preserved as *Wives* and they were to march up the river to meet "*Mr. Linkin*" bearing off as booty such things as they could carry. Notwithstanding all this, we are a brave and fearless people, and will meet this *emergency* as we expect to meet alothers, as become *men,* meting out justice to all in the fear of God.
    But I know [three lines illegible].

Remaining very respectfully your
Most Obet Servt
Jo. D. L. Davenport

Jo D. L. Davenport to Gov. [John J. Pettus], May 14, 1861, Governors Papers, Mississippi Department of Archives and History, printed in Winthrop D. Jordan, *Tumult and Silence at Second Creek: An Inquiry into a Civil War Conspiracy* (Baton Rouge: Louisiana State Univ. Press, 1993), 308–9.

A SLAVE'S VIEW OF RELIGION, EMANCIPATION, AND ABRAHAM LINCOLN

Friday Jones's autobiography is another of the few slave narratives that depict life during the Civil War. As with many slave narratives and contemporary memoirs by politicians and celebrities, Jones worked closely with an editor. The last page notes that "the author of this book is uncultured and unlearned—can neither read nor write."

Bretheren, what a blessing it is to dwell together in the spirit. Beware how you entertain a stranger, for you may entertain an angel. Have you forgotten the life we lived when we were slaves? Our sufferings were great, and in some places we were not allowed to worship God at all. We had to have secret prayer meetings on Saturday nights, and some would have to watch for the patrolmen and hard task-masters, to keep from being surprised, while the others prayed and sung. When the enemy was seen the watch would give the alarm; we would then close the meeting and make our escape, in order to keep our backs from being slashed and salted down.

In Marsh county, N. C., we had a noble speaker by the name of Minger Crudemp; he was the slave of a popular Baptist Minister, who, although he was a preacher, did not allow his slaves to worship the God he praised. This Minger Crudemp would hold prayer-meetings every Saturday night that he had a chance in spite of the penalty he would have to pay if he was caught; they would run him Saturday and Sunday. Bretheren, see how hard it was for us so serve God in the days of slavery. In some places they were allowed to praise God, but they had to have a white man to watch them. (When I was a small boy Bethey Thompson, a religious woman, was whipped by her mistress because she would pray and shout through the day.) Oh, how hard were the lives we led in those days. It was a common thing for slave men and women to run away into the woods to keep their masters from whipping them. To day, bretheren, we ought to love one another and be the best friends and citizens in America. Just look at the mercy of God in the midst of all the Presidents during slavery; yet we were held in bondage. God reared up Abraham Lincoln—one whom the people had not looked for—who used more power than any of the men in America. He caused the shackels to be thrown off the bondmen.

There are few of you who have ever thought what it cost to set you free—hundreds and thousands of lives were lost; even our greatest man, Abraham Lincoln, fell. No other man did the will of God as he did; it seemed as if he was intended to liberate us. He arose and declared that slavery should be abolished. This was power that God gave him. His heart failed him, but God pressed him on. All that we can do is to live close to the cross as a race. Life and blood was sacrificed for us; our people are gaining on one hand but losing on the other. Freedom of speech, to serve God, and to worship under our own vine and fig-tree, is ours.

Between sixty and seventy years ago the colored people of the South were shouting in the fields, when the overseer came and was about to whip them and drive them to work, when he was stricken down and converted by the power of God; then out came the master, and he was also converted. These I relate to show the power of God and the salvation of men and their souls.

How often have mortals been whipped to death and no one near to help or pity them. How horrible for a man to stand and sea his wife whipped and her wounds bathed in salt water, and not be able to protect her. To-day, some of our race are not doing much better.

Friday Jones, *Days of Bondage: Autobiography of Friday Jones, Being a Brief Narrative of His Trials and Tribulations in Slavery* (Washington, D.C.: Commercial Pub. Co., 1883). 17–18.

7

THE UNION REACTS TO RUNAWAY SLAVES
(TWO DOCUMENTS)

On May 24, 1861, three slaves escaped to the Union's Fortress Monroe in eastern Virginia. Their flight to freedom put their legal status up for public debate in the Union. Their master demanded that the men be returned under a prewar statute, the Fugitive Slave Law of 1850. Absurdly, a slaveholder in a state that had left the Union largely over slavery still demanded federal legal protection. At the fort, General Benjamin Butler described the men as "contraband," treating them as property seized from the enemy. As more fugitive slaves fled to his lines, Butler put them to work for wages. As contraband, their legal status was ambiguous: though no longer slaves, they were not yet legally free. In these two dispatches to his superiors Butler explained his initial reactions to escaped slaves.

HEADQUARTERS DEPARTMENT OF VIRGINIA,
Fort Monroe, May 24, 1861.
Lieutenant General [WINFIELD] SCOTT:

Saturday, May 25.

I had written thus far when I was called away to meet Major Cary, of the active Virginia volunteers, upon questions which here have arisen of very considerable importance both in a military and political aspect and which I beg leave to submit herewith.

On Thursday night three negroes, field hands belonging to Col. Charles K Mallory now in command of the secession forces in this district, delivered themselves up to my picket guard and as I learned from the report of the officer of the guard in the morning had been retained by him. I immediately gave personal attention to the matter and found satisfactory evidence that these men were about to be taken to Carolina for the purpose of aiding the secession forces there; that two of them left wives and children (one a free woman) here; that the other had left his master from fear that he would be called to take part in the rebel armies. Satisfied of these facts from cautious examination of each of the negroes apart from the others I determined for the present and until better advised as these men were very serviceable and I had great need of labor in my quartermaster's department to avail myself of their services, and that I would send a receipt to Colonel Mallory that I had so taken them as I would for any other property that was designed, adapted and about to be used against the United States.

As this is but an individual instance in a course of policy which may be required to be pursued with regard to this species of property I have detailed to the lieutenant-general this case and ask his direction. I am credibly informed that the negroes in this neighborhood are now being employed in the erection of batteries and other works by the rebels which it would be nearly or quite impossible to construct without their labor. Shall they be allowed the use of this property against the United States and we not be allowed its use in aid of the United States?

. . . Major Cary demanded to know with regard to the negroes what course I intended to pursue. I answered him substantially as I have written above when he desired to know if I did not feel myself bound by my constitutional obligations to deliver up fugitives under the fugitive-slave act. To this I replied that the fugitive-slave act did not affect a foreign country which Virginia claimed to be and that she must reckon it one of the infelicities of her position that in so far at least she was taken at her word; that in Maryland, a loyal State, fugitives from service had been returned, and that even now although so much pressed by my necessities for the use of these men of Colonel Mallory's yet if their master would come to the fort and take the oath of allegiance to the Constitution of the United States I would deliver the men up to him and endeavor to hire their services of him if he desired to part with them. To this Major Cary responded that Colonel Mallory was absent.

. . . Trusting that these dispositions and movements will meet the approval of the lieutenant-general and begging pardon for the detailed length of this dispatch, I have the honor to be, most respectfully, your obedient servant,

BENJ. F. BUTLER,
Major-General, Commanding

HEAD-QUARTERS DEPARTMENT OF VIRGINIA,
FORT MONROE, *May 27, 1861.*
Lieutenant-General [WINFIELD] SCOTT,

SIR:

Since I wrote my last dispatch the question in regard to slave property is becoming one of very serious magnitude. The inhabitants of Virginia are using their negroes in the batteries and are preparing to send the women and children south. The escapes from them are very numerous and a squad has come in this morning to my pickets bringing their women and children. Of course these cannot be dealt with upon the theory on which I designed to treat the services of able-bodied men and women who might come within my lines, and of which I gave you a detailed account in my last dispatch. Up to this time I have had come within my lines men and women with their children, entire families, each family belonging to the same owner. I have therefore determined to employ as I can do very profitably the able-bodied persons in the party, issuing proper food for the support of all and charging against their services the expense of care and maintenance of the non-laborers, keeping a strict and accurate account as well of the services as of the expenditure, having the worth of the services and the cost of the expenditure determined by a board of survey to be hereafter detailed. I know of no other manner in which to dispose of this subject and the questions connected therewith. As a matter of property to the insurgents it will be of very great moment, the number that I now have amounting as I am informed to what in good times would be of the value of $60,000. Twelve of these negroes I am informed have escaped from the batteries on Sewall's Point which this morning fired upon my expedition as it passed by out of range. As a means of offense therefore in the enemy's hands these negroes when able-bodied are of the last importance. Without them the batteries could not have been erected, at least for many weeks. As a military question and a question of humanity can I receive the services of a father and mother and not take the children? Of the humanitarian aspect I have no doubt; of the political one I have no right to judge.

Very respectfully, your obedient servant,
B. F. BUTLER

The War of the Rebellion: A Compilation of the Official Records of the Union and Confederate Armies (Washington, D.C.: Government Printing Office, 1880–1901), series 2, vol. 1, 752–54.

8

A NEWSPAPER EDITOR RELUCTANTLY
SUPPORTS SECESSION

William Woods Holden, the editor of the North Carolina Standard, *occupied center stage in some of the most fractious political debates on the Confederate home front. Holden saw himself as the voice of ordinary white men, especially those in the mountains of western North Carolina, which gave only lukewarm support for the Confederacy. In the immediate aftermath of Lincoln's election, Holden opposed North Carolina's exit from the Union. In this widely reprinted editorial, published in the wake of the attack on Fort Sumter, Holden voiced his belated support for secession.*

"We Must Fight!"

The proclamation of Mr. Lincoln has left to the people of the Border States no alternative but resistance or unconditional submission. The Southern man who would quietly submit to the doctrines enunciated in that document, is fit only for a slave. We do not go beyond that document, and it is not our purpose to go beyond it as long as this war shall last. We have labored for peace on honorable terms,—we should hail it now, on honorable terms, with profound satisfaction; but, much as we deprecate war, war must be *encountered,* and must be continued as long as the boot of a federal soldier rests on our soil.

It is true, the odds appear to be against us. The army and navy are in the hands of the old federal government. That government, too, has a name among the nations. It has the command of more ready means for offensive purposes in the way of money, men and arms than the South has; and the non-slaveholding States which uphold it have a common head around which to rally in their onset on the South. The latter section has but a small army—indeed, no regular army—and it has no navy. It has been one government of seven States unrecognized among the nations, and eight separate State governments making common cause with the former. But though the odds are against us, they are not near so great as that between England and the colonies. The slaveholding States can bring into their field one million of fighting men, as brave as ever charged bayonet or drew sword. These men are supported by those who remain at home, and by the labor of slaves. *The SOUTH can support and live within itself.* It can furnish itself with every article necessary for subsistence, and it wants no luxuries at a time like this. In addition to this our people will fight for Constitutional liberty against arbitrary power—for their homes and hearthstones, and, it may be, for existence. Such a people cannot be conquered. They may be overrun—their country may be laid waste, and their blood may flow like water, but they can no more be "subjugated" than the wind or the sea.

People of North Carolina! A call has been made for volunteers. Virginia and Maryland are encountering the first burst of the storm. . . . If we should keep the battle from our own doors we must unite with Virginia, Maryland, Kentucky, and Tennessee in offensive operations. A united and vigorous demonstration may lead to an honorable peace, but, failing in that, it will place us in line with an adequate force to sustain our sister States. The Confederate States will perform their whole duty. . . . The constituted authorities of the State have called; let our citizen soldiery answer. *They will!* One heretofore for peace and the Union comes forward to say to you that this is a just and honorable war. It is a war which could not have been avoided. It has been forced upon us. We must fight! Prove yourselves worthy of those who fought and fell at the Alamance and King's Mountain, and of those who, surviving, toiled and suffered through a seven year's war. Fanaticism and unjust power are on one side—"God and our native land" are on the other. And may He who rules the armies of heaven, and who disposes of men and nations, nerve every arm for the battle and give victory to those who are struggling for all they hold dear!

North Carolina Weekly Standard, April 24, 1861.

— 9 —

A NORTH CAROLINA MINISTER
ENDORSES THE WAR

Southern ministers had a great influence on public opinion during the Civil War era. Because churches published sermons and distributed them widely, religious ideas reached a wide audience. Church leaders played a crucial role in rallying citizens to support the war. North Carolina's Reverend Thomas Atkinson initially opposed secession. However, as the war broke out, he announced his support for the Confederate cause. While he gave this sermon to explain his support for the war, Atkinson still seemed uncertain about God's purpose in the crisis. Like many ministers, he feared that war would be the occasion for sin, as soldiers would be tempted to gamble and frequent prostitutes.

We stand to-day, face-to-face with civil war, a calamity, which, unless the experience and universal testimony of mankind deceive us, is direr and more to be deprecated than foreign war, than famine, than pestilence, than any other form of public evil. The cloud we have all been so long watching, which we have seen, day by day, and month by month, enlarging its skirts, and gathering blackness, is now beginning to burst upon us.

It seems to me that no one but an Atheist, or an Epicurean, can doubt that it is God who rides in this storm, and will direct the whirlwind, and that He now calls upon us to look to Him to consider our ways and our doings, to remember the offenses by which we have heretofore provoked Him, and to determine on the conduct we will hereafter pursue towards Him, toward our fellowmen and towards ourselves.

I feel that we have some solid grounds of encouragement to hope for His favour. This Commonwealth, with whose fortunes our own are linked, cannot be said to have any hand in causing, or precipitating the issue before us. She has sought, to the last moment, to avert it, and she has incurred censure by these efforts. But when compelled to elect between furnishing troops to subdue her nearest neighbors and kindred, and to open her Territory for the passage of armies marshalled to perform that odious, unauthorized and unhallowed object, or to refuse to aid, and to seek to hinder such attempts, she chose the part which affection, and interest and duty seems manifestly, and beyond all reasonable question, to require. What she has done, and is about to do, she does, as an old writer finely says in such a case, "willingly, but with an unwilling mind," as an imperative, but painful duty. Such is the temper, we may be well assured, in which it best pleases God, that strife of any sort, especially strife of this sort, should be entered on.

There is another consideration from which I derive great comfort, and which is certain to give comfort to all who receive it. It is that whatever we may think of some of the earlier steps in these disputes, yet as to the present questions between the North and the South, we can calmly, conscientiously, and, I think conclusively, to all impartial men, maintain before God and man that now at least we of the South are in the right. For we are on the defensive, we only ask to be let alone.

I cannot then doubt, and it seems a singular hallucination that any man should mistake, the righteous cause in this present most lamentable controversy, and I hope and I believe that God will bless with temporal success the righteous cause on the side of which one would desire to be found. Yet, however this thought may cheer us, we cannot disguise from ourselves that success, should we obtain it, will not probably be reached until an arduous and painful struggle, involving severe trials of the feelings, and of the character of the community, and of ourselves individually. And no man yet knows how he shall meet these trials. The most self-confident are usually the first to fall. "Let him not, that girdeth on his armour, boast himself as he who that taketh it off."

... And lastly, remember that you yourselves are now under trial; that the issues of that trial are for eternity, that though sharp it will be short; and if you endure it to the end you will be saved, and that the sharper the trial endured the more glorious will be the salvation. And now, dear brethren, what will be the result? Scripture prophecies it, and history prophecies it. Some of you will fail in this time of temptation, and will not endure it. Some of you, I fear, will sacrifice to the passions of the hour the Christian character, and the Christian hope. Some of you will come out of the trial purified and refined, and assured of a brighter crown. Resolve, oh Christian hearer, this day, in God's strength, to which class you will belong; whether to those who will cast away the crown to which perhaps for years they have aspired, or those who hold on to their hope with greater resolution than before.

Thomas Atkinson, D.D., "Christian Duty in the Present Time of Trouble: A Sermon Presented at St. James Church, On the Fifth Sunday after Easter, 1861" (Wilmington, N.C.: May 10, 1861), 6–8, 13.

10

A SOUTHERN WOMAN EMBRACES THE
CONFEDERATE CAUSE

Born into a privileged family, Virginia's Constance Harrison recalled the initial excitement with which many white Southern women embraced the Confederate cause. She enthusiastically rushed to view fighting in northern Virginia. Traveling without a male escort, Harrison, like many Confederate women, took advantage of new opportunities to achieve personal independence.

If we were to join her at all, wrote my mother from Bristoe Station, it must be now, as who knew when the military lines might shut us out? She warned me in an eloquent phrase that our sylvan paradise at Millwood must be exchanged for a poor little roadside tavern on the Orange and Alexandria Railroad, treeless, shabby, crowded to excess with officers' families, under burning sun all day, no ice but rather muddy water, no fruit, the plainest of fare, and nowhere to walk but up and down the railroad track. Per contra, the camp containing our boys was but five miles away; we should get all the army news direct; and day after day would see trains thundering by, full of eager soldiers, thrilling and shouting with joy that they were so near the goal! When the battle came we should be nearest it, to do our best for them. If our troops were to be driven back—why, then, we would "take our chance!"

We went. By lumbering stage-coach down the peaceful Shenandoah Valley, clad in the radiancy of summer foliage, by way-train here and there, passing "the Junction," the centre of all hopes and thoughts, the cradle of the future Army of Northern Virginia—arriving safely and gladly at Bristoe to "take our chance" with the others!

The month that elapsed before the first battle of the war, on July 18, 1861, was one in which I woke up to the strongest feeling of my young life. My mother saw her only remaining son, aged fifteen, looking several years younger, go into service as a marker in an Alexandria regiment. She sewed for him, with the neatest of stitches, white gaiters, and a "havelock" for his cap—these afterward abandoned by authority as too shining marks for riflemen—tears dropping now and then upon her handiwork, but never a thought of telling him he should not go. All about me were women ready to give their all. I realized that love of country can mean more than love of self.

In the family carriage, sold later as a superfluity of luxury to refugees and hospital nurses, we drove to several impromptu entertainments at Camp Pickens during the month of waiting the enemy's advance. What young girl's heart would not beat quicker in response to such an experience? There were dinners cooked and served to us by our soldier lads, spread upon rough boards, eaten out of tin plates and cups amid such a storm of the rollicking gayety and high hope that war seemed a merry pastime. In the infancy of war, the Louisiana chieftain, General Pierre Gustave Toutant Beauregard, of ancient Creole family, was distinctly looked upon as the future leader of the Confederacy. His name was upon all lips, his praise on every breeze that blew. Some early war rhymester wrote verses, of which the refrain was:

> Beau canon, Beauregard! Beau soldat, Beauregard!
> Beau sabruer! Beau frappeur! Beauregard!

Needless to say that to be received with visitors' honors at his headquarters was a source of undying pride. We met there the lamented Brigadier-General Bartow, killed at the first battle of Manassas; General Longstreet, who in those days, before he lost several children at once by scarlet fever, was rollicking and jolly always, looking, as his aide, Moxley Sorrel, afterwards said of him: "Like a rock of steadiness when sometimes in battle the world seemed flying to pieces"; and many another destined to high fame. There were drills, dress parades, and reviews, viewed from the headquarters tents of great generals. In all our dreams sounded the blare of trumpets, the roll of drums. And so till the morning of July 17, when word came that our troops were moving forward!

Now knew we the rude reality! Those women and girls and children left at Bristoe, who, on the 18th, spent all day on the railway tracks, straining eyes and ears in the direction of the belt of woodland above which arose columns of gun smoke, hearing the first guns of the war as distinctly as one hears a fog-horn on an Atlantic liner, had mostly all they loved best in the fight. It seemed eternal, that sullen roar of artillery, that crackle of fire-arms. And who should say how it was coming out? We could not rest; we could not speak or eat. Toward afternoon appeared, limping down a long, red clay road, a single, smoke-stained, fiery-faced bandaged soldier. With one accord the women fell upon him like a swarm of bees, questioned, fed, soothed, exalted him. He was rather a dreadful-looking person, we had to own, and his manner unpleasant, to say the least. His wound, on examination, proved a mere scratch on the middle finger, but he rose to the occasion as a hero, and answered our fevered, eager queries with statements that took our breath away.

Constance Harrison, *Refugitta of Richmond: The Wartime Recollections, Grave and Gay, of Constance Cary Harrison* (New York: Charles Scribner's Sons, 1916), 32–34.

11

MARK TWAIN'S "CAMPAIGN THAT FAILED"

At the beginning of the Civil War in 1861, Missouri remained in the Union, but it suffered from vicious guerrilla warfare between pro-Union forces and Confederate sympathizers. Before the state descended into guerrilla conflict, Samuel Clemens, who would later adopt the pen name of Mark Twain, joined an informally organized pro-Confederate militia in Hannibal, Missouri. After two weeks he left for Nevada, where he worked as a newspaper reporter. Although Twain's ironic sensibility surely influenced his account, so did his penchant for literary realism. This description of his experience effectively documents how he became disillusioned with the war.

You have heard from a great many people who did something in the war; is it not fair and right that you listen a little moment to one who started out to do something in it, but didn't? Thousands entered the war, got just a taste of it, and then stepped out again, permanently. These, by their very numbers, are respectable, and are therefore entitled to a sort of voice,—not a loud one, but a modest one; not a boastful one, but an apologetic one. They ought not to be allowed as much space as better people—people who did something—I grant that; but they ought at least to be allowed to state why they didn't do anything, and also to explain the process by which they didn't do anything. Surely this kind of light must have a sort of value.

I was visiting in the small town where my boyhood had been spent—Hannibal, Marion County. Several of us got together in a secret place by night and formed ourselves into a military company. One Tom Lyman, a young fellow of a good deal of spirit but of no military experience, was made captain; I was made second lieutenant.

We had no first lieutenant; I do not know why; it was a long time ago. There were fifteen of us. By the advice of an innocent connected with the organization, we called ourselves the Marion Rangers. . . .

Our scares were frequent. Every few days rumors would come that the enemy were approaching. In these cases we always fell back on some other camp of ours; we never stayed where we were. But the rumors always turned out to be false; so at last even we began to grow indifferent to them. One night a negro was sent to our corn-crib with the same old warning: the enemy was hovering in our neighborhood. We all said let him hover. We resolved to stay still and be comfortable. It was a fine warlike resolution, and no doubt we all felt the stir of it in our veins—for a moment. We had been having a very jolly time, that was full of horse-play and schoolboy hilarity; but that cooled down now, and presently the fast-waning fire of forced jokes and forced laughs died out altogether, and the company became silent. Silent and nervous. And soon uneasy—worried—apprehensive. We had said we would stay, and we were committed. We could have been persuaded to go, but there was nobody brave enough to suggest it. An almost noiseless movement presently began in the dark, by a general but unvoiced impulse. When the movement was completed, each man knew that he was not the only person who had crept to the front wall and had his eye at a crack between the logs. No, we were all there; all there with our hearts in our throats, and staring out toward the sugar troughs where the forest foot-path came through. It was late, and there was a deep woodsy stillness everywhere. There was a veiled moonlight, which was only just strong enough to enable us to mark the general shape of objects. Presently a muffled sound caught our ears, and we recognized it as the hoof-beats of a horse or horses. And right away a figure appeared in the forest path; it could have been made of smoke, its mass had such little sharpness of outline. It was a man on horseback; and it seemed to me that there were others behind him. I got hold of a gun in the dark, and pushed it through a crack between the logs, hardly knowing what I was doing, I was so dazed with fright. Somebody said "Fire!" I pulled the trigger. I seemed to see a hundred flashes and hear a hundred reports, then I saw the man fall down out of the saddle. My first feeling was of surprised gratification; my first impulse was an apprentice-sportsman's impulse to run and pick up his game. Somebody said, hardly audibly, "Good—we've got him! Wait for the rest!" But the rest did not come. We waited—listened—still no more came. There was not a sound, not the whisper of a leaf; just perfect stillness; an uncanny kind of stillness, which was all the more uncanny on account of the damp, earthy, late-night smells now rising and pervading it. Then, wondering, we crept stealthily out, and approached the man. He was lying on his back, with his arms abroad; his mouth was open and his chest heaving with long gasps, and his white shirt-front was all splashed with blood. The thought shot through me that I was a murderer; that I had killed a man—a man who had never done me any harm. That was the coldest sensation that ever went through my marrow. I was down by him in a moment, helplessly stroking his forehead; and I would have given anything then—my own life freely—to make him again what he had been five minutes before. And all the boys seemed to be feeling in the same way; they hung over him, full of pitying interest, and tried all they could to help him, and said all sorts of regretful things. They had forgotten all about the enemy; they thought only of this one forlorn unit of the foe. Once my imagination persuaded me that the dying man gave me a reproachful look out of his shadowy eyes, and it seemed to me that I would rather he stabbed me instead than done that. He muttered and mumbled like a dreamer in his sleep, about his wife and his child; and I thought with a new despair, "This thing that I have done does not end with him; it falls upon *them* too, and they never did me any harm, any more than he."

In a little while the man was dead. He was killed in war; killed in fair and legitimate war; killed in battle, as you may say; and yet he was as sincerely mourned by the opposing force as if he had been their brother. The boys stood there a half hour sorrowing over him, and recalling the details of the tragedy, and wondering who he might be, and if he were a spy, and saying that if it were to do over again they would not hurt him unless he attacked them first. It soon came out that mine was not the only shot fired; there were five others, a division of the guilt which was a grateful relief to me, since it in some degree lightened and diminished the burden I was carrying. There were six shots fired at once; but I was not in my right mind at the time, and my heated imagination had magnified my one shot into a volley.

The man was not in uniform, and was not armed. He was a stranger in the country; that was all we ever found out about him. The thought of him got to preying upon me every night; I could not get rid of it. I could not drive it away, the taking of that unoffending life seemed such a wanton thing. And it seemed an epitome of war; that all war must be just that—the killing of strangers against whom you feel no personal animosity; strangers whom, in other circumstances, you would help if you found them in trouble, and who would help you if you needed it. My campaign was spoiled. It seemed to me that I was not rightly equipped for this awful business; that war was intended for men, and I for a child's nurse. I resolved to retire from this avocation of sham soldiership while I could save some remnant of my self-respect. These morbid thoughts clung to me against reason; for at bottom I did not believe I had touched that man. The law of probabilities decreed me guiltless of his blood; for in all my small experience with guns I had never hit anything I had tried to hit, and I knew I had done my best to hit him. Yet there was no solace in the thought. Against a diseased imagination, demonstration goes for nothing. . . .

The thoughtful will not throw this war-paper of mine lightly aside as being valueless. It has this value: it is a not unfair picture of what went on in many and many a militia camp in the first months of the rebellion, when the green recruits were without discipline, without the steadying and heartening influence of trained leaders; when all their circumstances were new and strange, and charged with exaggerated terrors, and before the invaluable experience of actual collision in the field had turned them from rabbits into soldiers. If this side of the picture of that early day has not before been put into history, then history has been to that degree incomplete, for it had and has its rightful place there. There was more Bull Run material scattered through the early camps of this country than exhibited itself at Bull Run. And yet it learned its trade presently, and helped to fight the great battles later. I could have become a soldier myself, if I had waited. I had got part of it learned; I knew more about retreating than the man that invented retreating.

Mark Twain, "The Private History of a Campaign That Failed," *Century Magazine,* December 1885, 193–204.

12

A SLAVE DEBATES POLITICS
WITH HER OWNERS

Mattie J. Jackson, a former slave, was a teenager when the war began. She soon found herself in contested ground between Union and Confederate armies in Missouri. She escaped to Union lines before the war ended.

My mother and myself could read enough to make out the news in the papers. The Union soldiers took much delight in tossing a paper over the fence to us. It aggravated my mistress very much. My mother used to sit up nights and read to keep posted about the war. In a few days my mistress came down to the kitchen again with another bitter complaint that it was a sad affair that the Union had taken their delicate citizens who had enlisted and made prisoners of war of them—that they were babes. My mother reminded her of taking Fort Sumter and Major Anderson and serving them the same and that turnabout was fair play. She then hastened to her room with the speed of a deer, nearly unhinging every door in her flight, replying as she went that the Niggers and the Yankees were seeking to take the country. One day, after she had visited the kitchen to superintend some domestic affairs, as she pretended, she became very angry without a word being passed, and said—"I think it has come to a pretty pass, that old Lincoln, with his long legs, an old rail splitter, wished to put the Niggers on an equality with the whites; that her children should never be on an equal footing with a Nigger. She had rather see them dead." As my mother made no reply to her remarks, she stopped talking and commenced venting her spite on my companion servant. On one occasion Mr. Lewis searched my mother's room and found a picture of President Lincoln, cut from a newspaper, hanging in her room. He asked what she was doing with old Lincoln's picture. She replied it was there because she liked it. He then knocked her down three times, and sent her to the trader's yard for a month as punishment.

Mattie J. Jackson, *The Story of Mattie J. Jackson: Her Parentage, Experience of Eighteen Years in Slavery, Incidents During the War, Her Escape from Slavery: A True Story* (Lawrence, Mass.: Sentinel Office, 1866), 10–11.

13

A WHITE FAMILY WEIGHS THE
CONSEQUENCES OF WAR

Even families that favored the Confederacy hesitated to volunteer for the risks faced by soldiers. This letter was begun by Francis Glasgow, who lived in a rural county near Richmond, Virginia, but was finished by his wife, Anne Glasgow.

Although he supported the southern rebellion, Glasgow never fought in the war, but he did play an important role as manager of the Tredegar Iron Works in Richmond. The iron works produced rails and cannons, which were crucial to the survival of the Confederacy. The couple's daughter, Ellen, became a Pulitzer Prize-winning novelist and social critic.

My Dear Sister,

I rec'd your letter and we were glad to learn from home that you were all well, I have been unwell for a fortnight from an attack of disordered liver, but am now nearly recovered. We made a visit to Richmond yesterday and found Anna Junkin there with Willie. He has not improved as I had hoped, his symptoms are unfavorable and his friends quite uneasy. It seems that he will be confined a long time and they are very apprehensive that his leg will not heal and it is now too late to amputate. Poor fellow he has had a hard time of it, is much reduced since I last saw him, but is still apparently stout. The wound produces fever, and he has to be [illegible] at night by opium. I fear his physicians think the chances against him, but do not mention this where his family will hear it, as much more desperate cases than he have recovered. Uncle Frank had returned home a few days ago.

We have had a fine season and my crops are about as good as my land is capable of producing, which is not saying a great deal for them. There are spots in my corn field of very fine corn but if it will average 20 bus. per acre I will be satisfied. We have had vegetables and melons abundantly. We want to make our own cloth this year, but we find it expensive to have the wool carded and spun in the neighborhood and there are no factories in Richmond that will do it. They will buy the wool and pay a good price for it but they have large contracts and cannot give cloth in exchange for it. Are there not factories in your county that will take the wool and convert it into cloth for a certain sum per yard? It might be our best plan to send it to such a factory for carding + spinning they charge hear 2/3 per lb.

As Mr. Glasgow seems to have broken down in his letter writing I thought would try to finish it by adding a postscript. I feel ashamed dear Sister that I had not written to you long before this, but since parting from you I have not written to any one except occasionally a scribble [to] my precious brother whom I feel so much anxiety about. He is still at Fort Pickens, he writes quite often + says his labors as a physician are tenfold greater than when at home, but is willing to endure anything to serve his Country. You cannot imagine what I have suffered at the thought of Mr. Glasgow going into service. I knew it would be quite a sacrifice, for his health [illegible word] only admits of his attending to home duties, he has not been well for some time suffering from indigestion, seems better in the last few days and as the weather turns cool will I trust soon be well. Emily and Annie are both cooking some warm food this morning thinking it might do him good. Joseph has been sick more or less all summer from teething, is just getting his eye teeth now but as the weather is cooler sweet potatoes are at hand I hope he will not be much sick, he is a fine large boy very smart . . . + says almost any word + rides a stick horse all over the yard + is a terror to every cat + chicken to say nothing of Emmie and Annie whom he manages completely. Mammy and I have been busy picking wool but find it a tedious job. I have laid aside a pound for you, it seems to be very nice[.] I was anxious you should have it to knit yourself. I have been busy for some time pickling, putting up tomatoes + made some every nice ripe tomatoes + peach pickles. Wants to lend a bag of such things to the sick soldiers in a day or two.

I went to Richmond on Saturday, lucky one knew to bring something for the soldiers. There is a great deal of fever now among them the wounds known to produce it. Poor Willie Andrew, feel very anxious about him. Though his condition is so good he may be able to stand it. Dr. Cunningham was asked for his opinion + I heard Aunt Sally tell Anna that he said he might "weather it through, but in that event it would be a case of protracted + dire suffering. Mr. G got a letter from Robert a short time ago, we cannot feel thankful enough to God for his Great Mercy in sparing him through so much danger.

F. T. Glasgow and Anne Gholson Glasgow, Roslyn [Virginia], to Rebecca Glasgow, Green Forest [Virginia], August 25, 1861, Leyburn Library, Washington and Lee University.

14

SOUTH CAROLINA PLANTERS ABANDON
THE COASTLINE

*Even in the opening months of the war, slaveholders complained about
their fellow citizens' failure to make sacrifices to win the war. In a letter
to James Henry Hammond, a former U. S. senator and South Carolina
governor, his son, Harry Hammond, discusses his state's "low countrymen." The Lowcountry along the state's Atlantic coast included some
of the wealthiest men in the South. However, proximity to the ocean
made this area vulnerable to Union raids and possible slave rebellion.
Seeing their position as untenable, many Lowcountry slaveholders fled
from their plantations.*

Gardens Corner, 15th November 1861
Harry Hammond to James Henry Hammond

Dear Father,

I have been so busy that I have not had the time to write to you
before. . . . All over the Coossaw river has been abandoned to the enemy so that we are near them, but not on the track they will pursue.

You know probably as much about the state of affairs here as I
do, but you do not know perhaps what a miserable set these low
countrymen are. I think the war will sweep them out and I say there
will be no loss. They have fled like sheep leaving all their property in
the hands of the enemy, many without a change of clothes. No man
had the courage to burn his cotton or his house before he left—and
with one or two exceptions scarcely a negro has been saved. They
make no hesitation in saying that they will get pay for all this from
the Confederate government. Those who have saved anything are

selling it at the most extortionate prices to the troops. Here was Gov. Seabrook's son this morning—a man who was worth $100,000 a week ago—standing in his wagon and trying to sell a miserable marsh turkey, a rifle, and some turkey, to our common soldiers and all at the very highest market prices. And every day our contempt for such smallness overcomes the pity we feel for this panic stricken people. I am in the greatest want of horses. My business is suffering for it, and I may any day lose their full value for the lack of them. Besides if we have to make a rapid move I have nothing to depend on but my feet, which I would not complain of if it was not that I am required to look after many things which demand some more speedy form of locomotion. . . . But whoever brings them should have such a paper as would prevent them from being impressed by some foolish Militia officer. . . .

I wish you would write to me to Pocotaligo station putting my title and the 14th Reg S.C. V. on the letter. . . .

Give my love to all, Very affectionately,
Harry Hammond

From the James Henry Hammond Papers, Library of Congress, quoted in *The Secret and the Sacred: The Diaries of James Henry Hammond, a Southern Slaveholder,* ed. Carol Bleser (New York: Oxford Univ. Press, 1988), 281.

1862

15

"PRAYERS FOR FREEDOM": AN EX-SLAVE REMEMBERS THE WAR

During the Great Depression of the 1930s, the Works Progress Administration employed historians to conduct hundreds of interviews with former slaves. Published long after slavery's demise, these reminiscences must be approached skeptically. However, because they provide a rare glimpse of bondage from the perspective of slaves, they remain an invaluable resource. Interviewer David Hoggard originally recorded this interview in a stereotyped dialect form, as was then commonly done. To avoid such a condescending approach and to improve readability, the document is rendered here in standard English.

Mr. Charles Grandy, Ex-slave

February 26, 1937

The news of war, and the possibility of Negroes enlisting as soldiers, was truly a step closer to the answering of their prayers for freedom. Upon hearing of this good news Grandy joined a few of the others in this break for freedom. One night, he and a close friend packed a small quantity of food in a cloth and set out about midnight to join the northern army. Traveling at night most of the time, they were constantly confronted with the danger of being recaptured. Successfully eluding their followers, they reached Portsmouth after many narrow escapes. From Portsmouth they moved to Norfolk. Grandy and his friend decided to take different routes of travel. . . . While picking berries along a ditch bank, he was hailed by a Yankee soldier, who, having come in contact with runaway slaves before, greeted him friendly, and questioned of him his home and his knowledge of work. He was taken to camp and assigned as a cook. At first he was not very successful in his job, but gradually improvement was shown. He was asked what wages he would accept. It was such a pleasure to know that he had escaped the clutches of slavery, he did not ask for wages; but instead, he was willing to work for anything they would give him, no matter how small, as long as he didn't have to return to slavery.

Within a short period he was given a uniform and gun and was fully enlisted as a soldier, in the 19th regiment of Wisconsin, Company E. Here he remained in service until November, 1862, after which time he returned to Norfolk to spend some time with his mother, who was still living. While sitting in the doorway one day, with his mother, he was again confronted with the proposition of reenlisting. He agreed to do so for one year, to serve as a guard at Fortress Monroe. He remained there until the close of the war, offering brave and skillful services.

Mr. Grandy is now ninety-five years old, residing at 609 Smith Street, Norfolk, Virginia. He is still able to attend the various conventions of Civil War veterans. He can read, write, and has a fair knowledge of the Bible. His main interest is the organization of Negroes into strong groups. He enjoys talking about religion and is quite an interesting and intelligent person to talk with.

Slave Narratives: A Folk History of Slavery in the United States From Interviews with Former Slaves, vol. 17, *Virginia Narratives,* Typewritten Records Prepared by the Federal Writers' Project, Work Projects Administration for the District of Columbia, Sponsored by the Library of Congress (Washington, D.C.: Works Progress Administration, 1941), 21–23, available online at "Born in Slavery: Slave Narratives from the Federal Writer's Project, 1936–1938," https://memory.loc.gov/ammem/snhtml/mesnbibVolumes1.html.

16

CONSCRIPTION AND THE CONFEDERACY:
A VIEW FROM SOUTH CAROLINA

In 1862 the Confederacy began a national military draft. No issue caused more friction between states and the national government, as state governments sought to retain home defense forces to suppress potential slave rebellions. In South Carolina, which had a slave majority, whites sought exemptions for militia service.

DEPARTMENT OF THE MILITARY
Columbia, S. C., April 30, 1862.
Hon. G. W. RANDOLPH,
Secretary of War, Richmond, Va.:

SIR:

I have the honor to enclose for your consideration an official copy of a resolution passed by the Governor and Council of this State. I send with it, as the basis of the action, a communication from General Jones, chairman of the Board of Visitors of the State Military Academy. These papers sufficiently explain the object and reason of this letter, and I will add a very few observations: The students of the academy are always ready, being well officered, organized, armed, and equipped. We have always held them as a most sufficient reserve, and if the occasion should require they will be far more effective organized as they are than they could be if thrown out separately and absorbed in the various corps of the Army. I earnestly hope that it may be consistent with your views on policy to issue very soon an order giving effect to the request of the Governor and Council in this particular.

There is another subject to which I beg leave to call your attention, and it is certainly not of less importance than the other. The act which provides for exemptions from service under the late conscription law of Congress does not embrace one of the most important classes of our people. The masters or owners of negroes in this State are, for the most part, now in the Army. Before going they had provided themselves with proper overseers for the management of the slaves and for the production of their material supplies, without which not only our people but our armies must perish. If the overseers should now be taken, the agricultural industry of this State must be immeasurably damaged and diminished. Substitutes for them, when they are within the conscriptive age, cannot be obtained. The men are not to be had, for they are not in the country, but in the army or the workshops or manufactories. In view of all of this, permit me, therefore, to make the following suggestions: An order stating that in any case where an overseer or manager of slaves between the ages of eighteen and thirty-five has been exempt from the military service by the law of the state in which he resides, he shall be, and hereby, assigned to the duty in which he is now engaged, without pay from the Confederate Government, until further orders. This will accomplish the object and leave it again under your control. . . .

JAMES CHESNUT, Jr.,
Chief, & c.

The War of the Rebellion: A Compilation of the Official Records of the Union and Confederate Armies (Washington, D.C.: Government Printing Office, 1880–1901), series 4, vol. 1, 1106.

17

A LOUISIANA FAMILY FLEES FROM
THE UNION ARMY

At the outset of the war Kate Stone was twenty years old. She lived at Brokenburn, a cotton plantation in Louisiana, with five brothers, a young sister, and her mother, a widow. Her family owned 1,260 acres of land and about 150 slaves. In addition to its depiction of slavery, Stone's journal describes a relatively neglected subject: the experience of Confederate refugees.

June 29. [1862]

Brother Walter brought a letter from My Brother to Mamma. It was sent by Tom Manlove, who is at home on sick leave. In the letter he is despondent and homesick and very anxious about us all now that the enemy is at our very doors. He says that it will kill him to remain idle in Virginia when we are in such danger and that he must come back to see about us and fight in the Mississippi army. He seems so desperate. We fear he will do something rash and get into trouble. He cannot realize that we are safe enough for the present.

We hear today that the Yankees are impressing all the Negro men on the river places and putting them to work on a ditch which they are collecting across the point opposite Vicksburg above DeSoto. They hope to turn the river through there and to leave Vicksburg high and dry, ruining that town and enabling the gunboats to pass down the river without running the gauntlet of the batteries at Vicksburg. They have lately come up as far as Omega, four miles from us, taking the men from Mr. Noland's place down. We hear several have been shot attempting to escape. We were satisfied there would soon be outrages committed on private property. Mamma had all the men on the place called up, and she told them if the Yankees came on the place each Negro must take care of himself and run away and hide. We think they will.

From a late paper we see that Butler is putting his foot down more firmly [in New Orleans] every day. A late proclamation orders every man in the city to take the oath of allegiance. There will be the most severe penalties in case of refusal. Butler had Mr. Mumford, a gentleman of New Orleans, hung over the mint. The most infamous order and murder of which only Butler is capable. Is the soul of Nero reincarnated in the form of Butler? Why can he not fall of the scourge of New Orleans, yellow fever?

Gen. Breckenridge started to Vicksburg yesterday in a carriage, and he runs great risk of being captured, as they have packets across the point. Several of our soldiers have been taken trying to make their way across there. Brother Walter slipped through just in time.

The drought was broken last night by a good rain and the planters are feeling better. This insures a good corn crop and it was beginning to suffer. It is so essential to make good food crops this year. When we heard the cool drops splashing on the roof, "We thanked God and took fresh courage." Such a lovely morning. It is a pleasure to breathe the soft, cool air and look out over the glad, green fields, flashing and waving in the early sunlight.

June 30. [1862]

The excitement is very great. The Yankees have taken the Negroes off all the places below Omega, the Negroes generally going most willingly, having been promised their freedom by the vandals. The officers coolly go on the places, take the plantation books, and call off the names of all the men they want, carrying them off from their masters without a word of apology. They laugh at the idea of payment and say of course they will never send them back. A good many planters are leaving the river and many are sending their Negroes to the back country. We hope to have ours in a place of greater safety by tomorrow. . . .

All on this place, Negroes and whites, are much wrought up. Of course, the Negroes do not want to go, and our fear is when the Yankees come and find them gone they will burn the buildings in revenge. They are capable of any horror. We look forward to their raid with great dread. Mrs. Savage sent for her silver today. We have been keeping it since the gunboats came. They will all leave in two days for Bayou Macon. Would like to see them before they get off.

Mamma has been in bed all day. Sister is suffering with a large rising on her leg and Brother Walter from a severe cold. He is spitting blood, all yesterday and today, and tomorrow is compelled to go on a long trip. We have been arranging everything for an early start.

John Q. Anderson, ed., *Brokenburn: The Journal of Kate Stone, 1861–1868* (Baton Rouge: Louisiana State Univ. Press, 1955), 125–27, 129.

—— 18 ——

THE PRISON DIARY OF A
TENNESSEE UNIONIST

William "Parson" Brownlow edited a Tennessee newspaper, The Whig.
*Until Confederate authorities suspended its publication in the fall of
1861, it was the largest antiwar publication in the South. After being
arrested for his political views in December 1861, he kept a journal
of the time he spent in jail. Confederate secretary of war Judah P.
Benjamin authorized his deportation to Union lines in March 1862.
Brownlow's description of "insolent Southern negroes" in uniform
is especially striking. Historians have found only a very few cases of
blacks serving as Confederate soldiers, although some slaves worked
in Confederate camps to build fortifications or to work as personal
servants to officers.*

Here my jail-journal commences, written in prison, with a lead
pencil, in small blank-books I kept in my side pocket. I will give
it, without any polish or the slightest improvement, just as it was
sketched—written amidst the crowd and clamor of so many men,
some sick, others impatient and tired, but all respectful to me and
kind to each other.

Tuesday, Dec. 10. [1861]
The tedium of prison-life has rather oppressed us all to-day. It has
been relieved a little by our coming in contact with some insolent
Southern negroes. One in uniform, from Alabama, has been guarding us with a double-barreled shot-gun, and has been insulting and
abusive. Another negro came into the jail and threw slugs of lead
through the gates into the iron cage of one of our prisoners. We all

have to submit to this sort of treatment. When we are put here, we have been deprived of our weapons, pocket-knives and money and all are confiscated, leaving us helpless. Some of our men had several hundred dollars in their pockets, and all had more or less money.

Wednesday, Dec. 11. [1861]

C. A. Haun, a man about twenty-seven years of age, was taken out today and hung, on a charge of bridge-burning. He had but a short notice of his sentence, having been condemned without any defence allowed him by a drum-head and whiskey drinking court martial. I think that he was notified of his coming death about one hour in advance. I know he desired a Methodist preacher sent for to pray and sing with him, and this was refused him: so that he was forced to exchange worlds without the "benefit of clergy." They drove up a cart with a coffin in it, surrounded by a hardened set of Rebel troops, displaying their bayonets and looking and talking savagely. It is stated to us that one of the Rebel chaplains officiated at the hanging, and stated that Haun desired him to say that he had been misled by the Union leaders and papers, and was sorry for his conduct, whereupon Haun contradicted him, and said that he admitted no such thing. Haun leaves a young wife and two or three little children. I had, myself, sooner be Haun than any one of his murderers.

Fifteen more prisoners came in today from Greene and Hancock counties, charged with having been Union men, and accustomed to drill, which I have no doubt is true. What their fate will be, God only knows. These savage beasts of the Southern Confederacy are prepared to hang a man for saying that secession is wrong or unconstitutional, although John C. Calhoun admitted that much himself.

Saturday, Dec. 14. [1861]

Three more prisoners from the upper counties were brought in to-day. They speak of the outrages perpetrated by these Rebel troops, and of their murderous spirit. Three officers visited me to-day. Lieutenant-Colonel [Edward] Golladay stated to me that, whilst he was not informed as to what they would do with me, he was in favor of sending me to Nashville, boarding me at a hotel, giving me the privileges of the city until the war was over, but confining me to its limits. I told him that his mode of punishment was not severe, but that I preferred his Government should carry out the stipulations with me and send me beyond their limits.

General [William Henry] Carroll visited me, but was, as I supposed, more drunk than usual. He thought that I ought to be out of this, but that I ought to be willing to swear allegiance to the Confederate government. I told him I would lie here until I died with old age before I would take such an oath. I did not consider that he had a Government; I regarded it as a big Southern mob. It had never been recognized by any Government on earth, and never would be.

W. G. Brownlow, *Sketches of the Rise, Progress, and Decline of Secession, with a Narrative of Personal Adventures among the Rebels* (Philadelphia: George W. Childs, 1862), 307, 311–12, 316–17.

19

THE GOVERNOR OF GEORGIA
DENOUNCES THE DRAFT

*Governor Joseph Brown of Georgia played a critical role in leading the
secession of his state. Always a contentious figure, Brown soon became
a thorn in the side of the Confederate government. While publicly
declaring his loyalty to the cause, he denounced plans for conscription. He saw Confederate legislation on the draft as the first national
conscription in American history and a violation of the Confederate
Constitution. He sent this letter to President Jefferson Davis.*

Milledgeville, Ga.
May 8, 1862

Dear Sir:

I have the honor to acknowledge the receipt of your favor of
the 28th ult., in reply to my letter to you upon the subject of the
Conscription Act. I should not trouble you with a reply, were it not
that principles are involved of the most vital character, upon the
maintenance which, in my opinion, depend not only the rights and
sovereignty of the States, but the very existence of State Government.

While I am always happy as an individual to render you any assistance in my power . . . and while I am satisfied you will bear testimony that I have never, as the executive of this State, failed in a single
instance to furnish all the men, and more than you have called for,
and to assist you with all the other means at my command, I cannot
consent to commit the State to a policy which is, in my judgment,
subversive of her sovereignty, and at war with all the principles for
the support of which Georgia entered into this revolution.

It may be said that this is no time to discuss constitutional questions in the midst of revolution, and that State rights and State sovereignty must yield for a time to the higher law of necessity. If this is a safe principle of action, it cannot certainly apply until the necessity is shown to exist; and I apprehend it would be a dangerous policy to adopt were we to admit that those who are to exercise the power of setting aside the Constitution, are to be the judges of the necessity for so doing. . . .

Feeling satisfied that the Conscription Act, and such other Acts of Congress as authorize the President to appoint or commission the officers of the militia of the State, when employed in the service of the Confederate States "to repel invasion," are in palpable violation of the Constitution, I can consent to do no act which commits Georgia to willing acquiescence in their binding force upon her people. I cannot therefore consent to have anything to do with the enrollment of the conscripts in this State; nor can I permit any commissioned officer of the militia to be enrolled, who is necessary to enable the State to exercise her reserved right of training her militia, according to the discipline prescribed by Congress, at a time, when to prevent trouble with her slaves, a strict military police is absolutely necessary to the safety of her people. Nor can I permit any other officer, civil or military, who is necessary to the maintenance of the State Government, to be carried out of the State as a conscript.

Your obedient servant,
Joseph E. Brown

Joseph Brown to Jefferson Davis, May 8, 1862, in *Confederate Records of the State of Georgia,* vol. 3, ed. Allen D. Candler (Atlanta: Charles B. Byrd, 1910), 212–21.

20

THE UNION'S ATTACK ON RICHMOND IN 1862: A VIEW FROM WITHIN THE CITY

Before the war, Judith McGuire of Alexandria, Virginia, was a member of an affluent family. She left her home after Federal occupation forces overran the town in May 1861.

As fighting raged just outside Richmond in the 1862, McGuire followed rumors and newspaper reports, which could be unreliable. The immediate crisis receded when the Confederates triumphed in the Seven Days' Battles, in which they thwarted a Union campaign to capture the city. In the passage below, McGuire noted the terrible human cost of the fighting.

June 27th. [1862]
10 o'clock at Night.

Another day of great excitement in our beleaguered city. From early dawn the cannon has been roaring around us. Our success has been glorious! The citizens—gentlemen as well as ladies—have been fully occupied in the hospitals. Kent, Paine & Co. have thrown open their spacious building for the use of the wounded. Gen. C., of Texas, volunteer aide to General [John Bell] Hood, came in from the field covered with dust, and slightly wounded; he represents the fight is terrible beyond example. The carnage is frightful. General [Stonewall] Jackson has joined General Lee, and nearly the whole army on both sides were engaged. The enemy has retired before our troops to their strong works near Gaines's Mill. Brigade after brigade of our brave men were hurled against them, and repulsed in disorder. General Lee was heard to say to General Jackson, "The fighting is desperate; can our men stand it?" Jackson replied, "General, I know our boys—they will never go back." In a short time a large part of our force was brought up in one grand attack, and then the enemy was utterly routed. Gen. C. represents the valour of Hood and his brigade in the liveliest colours, and attributes the grand success at the close of the day greatly to their extraordinary gallantry. The works were the strongest ever seen in the country, and General C. says that the armies of the world could not have driven our men from them.

Another bulletin from the young surgeon of the Fortieth [Virginia Infantry Regiment]. That noble regiment has lost heavily—several of the "Potomac Rifles" among the slain—sons of old friends and acquaintances. Edward Brockenbrough, dreadfully wounded, has been brought in, and is tenderly nursed. Our own boys are mercifully spared. Visions of the battle-field have haunted me all day. Our loved ones, whether friends or strangers—all Southern soldiers are dear to us—lying dead and dying; the wounded in the hot sun, the dead being hastily buried. [George] McClellan is said to be retreating. "Praise the Lord, O my soul!"

[June] *28th.*

The casualties among our friends, so far, not very numerous. My dear R. T. C. [Raleigh T. Colston] is here, slightly wounded; he hopes to return to his command in a few days. Colonel Allen, of the Second Virginia, killed. . . . But what touches me most clearly is the death of my young friend, Clarence Warwick, of this city. Dearly have I loved that warm-hearted, high-minded, brave boy, since his early childhood. To-night I have been indulging sad memories of his earnest manner and affectionate tones, from his boyhood up; and now what must be the shock to his father and brothers, and to those tender sisters, when to-morrow the telegraph shall tell them of their loss! His cousin, Lieutenant-Colonel Warwick, is desperately wounded. Oh, I pray that his life may be spared to his poor father and mother. He is so brave and skillful an officer that we cannot spare him, and how can they? The booming of the cannon still heard distinctly, but the sound is more distant.

June 30.

McClellan certainly retreating. We begin to breathe more freely; but he fights as he goes. Oh, that he may be surrounded before he gets to his gun-boats! Rumours are flying about that he is surrounded; but we do not believe it—only hope that he may be before he reaches the river. The city is sad, because of the dead and dying, but our hearts are filled with gratitude and love. The end is not yet—oh that it were!

Judith W. McGuire, *Diary of a Southern Refugee during the War, by a Lady of Virginia* (New York: E. J. Hale and Son, 1868), 125–26; 249–50.

21

THE ARREST OF A VIRGINIA DISSENTER

A native of New Jersey with strong proslavery beliefs, John B. Jones moved to the Confederacy as the conflict began. He became a clerk employed by the Confederate War Department. In spite of his political bias, he was a perceptive observer and produced an unusually valuable diary.

May 2d (1862).

An iniquitous-looking prisoner was brought in to-day from Orange C. H., by the name of Robert Stewart. The evidence against him is as follows: He is a Pennsylvanian, though a resident of Virginia for a number of years, and owns a farm in Orange County. Since the series of disasters, and the seeming downward progress of our affairs, Stewart has cooled his ardor for independence. He has slunk from enrollment in the militia, and under the Conscription Act. And since the occupation of Fredericksburg by the enemy he has made use of such equivocal language as to convince his neighbors that his sympathies are wholly with the Northern invader.

A day or two since, near nightfall, three troopers, weary and worn, halted at Stewart's house and craved food and rest for themselves and horses. Stewart, supposing them to be Confederate soldiers, declared he had nothing they wanted, and that he was destitute of every description of refreshments. They said they were sorry for it, as it was a long ride to Fredericksburg.

"Are you *Union* soldiers?" asked Stewart, quickly.

"Yes," said they, "and we are on scouting duty."

"Come in! Come in! I have everything you want!" cried Stewart, and when they entered he embraced them.

A sumptuous repast was soon on the table, but the soldiers refused to eat! Surprised at this, Stewart demanded the reason; the troopers rose, and said they were Confederate soldiers, and it was their duty to arrest a traitor. They brought him hither. Will he, too, escape merited punishment?

John B. Jones, *A Rebel War Clerk's Diary,* vol. 1 (Philadelphia: Lippincott and Co., 1866), 122.

22

A BLACK ABOLITIONIST ON TEACHING
FORMER SLAVES

Abolitionist Charlotte Forten, a native of Philadelphia, began her formal education in Salem, Massachusetts, in 1854, where she was the only black student in a class of two hundred. After Union troops liberated the coastal sea islands of South Carolina, the white population fled, leaving behind a black majority population that had previously been barred from learning to read and write. In 1862, Forten became the first black teacher in this new community. By writing about the experience, she helped debunk the myth of African American intellectual inferiority.

St. Helena's Island, on which I am, is about 6 miles from the main land of Beaufort. I must tell you that we were rowed hither from Beaufort by a crew of Negro boatmen, and that they sung for us several of their own beautiful songs. There is a peculiar wildness and solemnity about them which cannot be described, and the people accompany me singing with a singular swaying motion of the body, which seems to make it more effective. We sang that John Brown song with spirit, as we drove through the pines and palmettos. Ah, it was good to be able to sing that here, in the very heart of Rebeldom!

There are no white soldiers on this island. It is protected by gunboats, and by negro pickets who do their duty well. These men attacked and drove back a boat-load of rebels who tried to land here one night, several weeks ago. General [Rufus] Saxton is forming a colored regiment at Beaufort and many of the colored men from this and the adjacent islands have joined it. The General is a noble-hearted man, who has a deep interest in the people here, and he is generally loved and trusted by them. I am sorry to say that some other officers treat the freed people and speak of them with the greatest contempt. They are consequently disliked and feared.

As far as I have been able to observe—and although I have not been here long, I have seen and talked with many of the people—the negroes here seem to be, for the most part, an honest, industrious, and sensible people. They are eager to learn; they rejoice in their new-found freedom. It does one good to see how *jubilant* they are over the downfall of their "secesh" masters, as they call them. I do not believe there is a man, woman, or even a child that is old enough to be sensible, that would submit to being made a slave again. There is evidently a deep determination in their souls that *that* shall never be. Their hearts are full of gratitude to the Government and to the "Yankees." . . .

There are two ladies in the school beside myself—Miss T. and Miss M., both of whom are most enthusiastic teachers. They have done a great deal of good here. At present, our school is small, many of the children on the island being ill with whooping cough—but in general it averages eighty or ninety. I find the children generally well-behaved, and eager to learn; yea, they are nearly almost all eager to learn, and many of them make most rapid improvement. It is a great happiness to teach them. I wish some of those persons at the North, who say the race is hopelessly and naturally inferior, could see the readiness with which these children, so long oppressed and deprived of every privilege, learn and understand.

I have some grown pupils—people on our own plantation—who take their lessons in the evenings. It will amuse you to know that one of them—our-man-of-all work—is named *Cupid*. (Venuses and Cupids are very common here.) He told me he was "feared" he was almost too old to learn; but I assured him that was not the case, and now he is working diligently at the alphabet. One of my people—Harry—is a scholar to be proud of. He makes a most wonderful improvement. I never saw anyone so determined to learn. I enjoy hearing human Cupids talk about the time that the rebels had to flee from this place. The remembrance of it is evidently a source of the most exquisite happiness and amusement. There are several families living here, and it is very pleasant to visit their cabins and talk with them. They are very happy now. They never weary of contrasting their present with their former condition, and they work for the Government now, and receive wages and rations in return. I am very happy here, but wish I was able to do a great deal more. I wish some one would write a little Christmas hymn for our children to sing. I want to have a kind of festival for them on Christmas, if we can. The children have just learned the John Brown song, and next week they are going to learn the song of the "Negro Boatman." The little creatures love to sing. They sing with the greatest enthusiasm. I wish you could hear them.

Charlotte Forten, in *The Liberator,* December 12, 1862.

ANDREW JOHNSON AND POLITICAL CONFLICT IN TENNESSEE (TWO DOCUMENTS)

Tennessee's Andrew Johnson is best known as the first U. S. president to be impeached. But in 1861 he was the only senator from a Confederate state to oppose secession. During the secession crisis Johnson risked his life by returning to his home state to build Union support. As Federal troops moved further to the South in 1862, Abraham Lincoln appointed Johnson the military governor of Tennessee. A former tailor, Johnson had long resented the political power and prestige wielded by wealthy planters, but he shared their racism. In 1862 he received this petition from prisoners suspected of disloyalty to the Union.

Nashville Sept 2/62.
Petition from Workhouse Prisoners
To His Exelency
Andrew Johnson, Gov &c.

The undersigned, petitioners, most respectfully Show your Honor, That they are now confined in the workhouse of the City of Nashville as political prisoners, caused to be taken and imprisoned, by the order and direction of General [Richard W.] Johnson. They are informed that they have been turned over to Your Exelency for examination and trial.

Therefore by virtue of the powers in you vested, and relying upon your known clemency & mercy, and in pursuant to your powers of parden, to those that have errd, we appeal in mercy, those of us that have upon our returning to loyalty, to parden and set us at liberty, upon our taking the usual oath, & giving such bond as may be requred, which we are ready to do. some of us are already loyal & have done nothing to our knowledg to warrant our confinement, supose we were arrested under a supposed State of fact, but which in fact are erroneous. we subjoin a Statement of facts which are true & which we defy refutation. The Statement marked Exhibit A & made apart of this petition. . . .

Will you please have us brought out as, conveant, and examined, and if found wirthy dischagd upon such terms, as in your wisdom & mercy may see fit, to-day if you please.

As in duty bound they will ever pray &c.

Thirty-two signers, and their attorney, Manson M. Brien

Endangered by partisan warfare, these Tennessee civilians asked Johnson for aid in fighting against Confederate loyalists in their vicinity.

From Anonymous
Private and Confidential
Nashville, October '62
To His Excellency
Gov. Andrew Johnson

Dear Sir.

A gentleman who knows you well remarked to me not long since that you had kinder feelings towards the people than any one exercising military authority in Nash[ville.] I am also informed that you are opposed to soldiers going about through the country *pillaging & plundering* the people. War is horrid enough when viewed in any light, but when waged with savage cruelty, it is unworthy a civilized or Christian people. As a friend of the people—I appeal to you to do every thing in your power as Brigadar General and Military *Governor* to mitigate their sufferings. Your object is I believe to put down the rebellion and restore Tennessee to her former position in the Union—

but in doing this you do not wish to heap in injustice and wrong upon the people. The late foraging expeditions from the city—have caused a great deal of suffering. . . .

Federal soldiers sent out to get forage & provisions—have entered *private houses* and robbed *peacable—unoffending* citizens of their clothing—bed clothing Household furniture etc. . . . . in numbers of instances—Women have been insulted, and some robbed of their Jewelry—I know one man who voted the Union ticket 9 Feb. 1861, who says he did *not vote* for separation or secession June 8/61, and who has all along remained a quiet *good* citizen—he has *fed* hundreds of federal soldiers—although he has a protection he has been robbed of hundred of dollars in provisions—his wife insulted—& He has borne it with the patience of Job—I advised him to go to you . . . and that *you would have him protected.* This wholesale plundering and pillaging through the country while it causes great suffering among the people drives thousands to desperation, and causes a great many to enter the southern army—will also greatly *demoralize* the Federal soldiers—

I fully concur with you in your sentiments that "the soul of *liberty* is the love of *law*[.]" I also endorse the sentiment of your speech in Dec '60 "I believe the continuance of slavery—depends upon the preservation of this Union, and a compliance with all the guarantees of the Constitution"—Thousands who went into secession for lost rights in the Territories, may now exclaim what has become of my rights in the states—Secession was the worst remedy that could have been resorted to—& thousands now see their error[.] I was in Tenn—most of the time during the progress of the revolution (for all must *now be* satisfied that peaceable secession was a humbug . . . and I know that thousands and tens of thousands voted for secession or revolution, through error of judgment. They did not intend to do wrong—but were carried away by the *excitement* and *madness*—of the *hour.* I appeal to you in *behalf* of this class of *people*[.] *Save them* from the consequences of their own folly or *madness* if you *please*—Has it not occurred to you, in the last *18* months or 2 *years,* that for *one crazy man* in a *Lunatic asylum*—there are hundreds if not *thousands running at large*—There can be a species of Secession or *proslavery* madness as well as abolition fanaticism[.] . . . Thousands of men who delighted to elevate you to power and office—have been led to their own *ruin*—a good deal through their sympathies for the south, and from error of judgment—

Private and Confidential

[*Johnson endorsed this letter: "To be preserved—in reference to the people &c—."*]

Leroy B. Graf and Ralph W. Haskins, eds., *The Papers of Andrew Johnson,* vol. 6, *1862–1864* (Knoxville: Univ. of Tennessee Press, 1983), 6–7, 15–18.

24

REMEMBERING THE DEATH OF A
CONFEDERATE SOLDIER

A Presbyterian minister and theologian, Robert Lewis Dabney taught at Hampden-Sydney College in Virginia. He briefly served on the staff of his friend General Thomas "Stonewall" Jackson in 1862. The scholar, unsuited for military life, proved to be a poor officer at the Seven Days' Battles outside Richmond in 1862. He returned home after four months of service, citing a "camp disease." He never returned to active duty. In this eulogy for the funeral of Confederate soldier Abram C. Carrington, Dabney struggled to make sense of God's purpose in bringing such a destructive war.

Death, and especially what men call a premature death, must ever be regarded by us as a great natural evil. If I should profess to be, myself, or should demand of you, to be insensible to it, you would justly consider me as guilty of cant. The very instinct of man's animal nature abhors it, and his earthly affections shudder at the severance which it effects between them and their dear objects. So, the death of friends cannot but be a felt bereavement to survivors, be its circumstances what they may. But it has ever appeared to me that in the fall of the Christian in battle there was more to mitigate the stroke, and to overcome death by the victory more triumphant consolation than in any other by which the good man meets his fate. The unreflecting may be startled by this assertion. They think of all the externals of death on the battle field; of the ghastly forms in which the destroyer comes, of the corpse prone upon its mother earth, begrimed perhaps with sweat, and dust of the conflict; of the burial in which he is taken fresh and gory from the field, his breast unconfined by coffin or winding-sheet, and shrouded only in his martial cloak; and of the nameless grave where he sleeps alone in his blood. All this is pictured in contrast with the solemn decencies of those funeral rites which affection renders, in more peaceful seasons, with a sort of mournful delight. They afflict themselves with the thought that no friend was near to minister to his pangs, no saintly man of God to calm the agitation of his soul by his prayers, no mother or wife to receive his last farewell; but his dying groans found no echo but the thunders of the receding battle.

Well, all these things are true; too often, alas, have I seen them verified: but they are true as elements of pain only to the survivors. The dying hero feels them not. Here is our illusion; that we cheat our sorrow into the belief [that] these ministrations of affection reach the insensible clay; when in truth, they only solace our own bereaved affection. Death is always a solitary struggle. However we *may be* surrounded by friends, when the shadow of the great agony falls upon us, it shuts us out like a dark veil from their aid, and we must meet the last enemy alone. And however the neglect of the beloved remains may harrow the feelings of those who loved him, the departed is all unconscious of it. On the other hand is it nothing, that he is translated to his reward by a sudden and painless stroke? He feels one electric shock, as the deadly missile smites him, and then, the very capacity for pain is benumbed, and wakes no more, till he awakes in the world where pain is unknown. He has no share in the long tortures of wearying sickness, or the mortifying decay of age: he feels none of the anxious forebodings, the hope deferred waning into sickening despair, by which the more peaceful bed of disease is haunted. Death casts none of its shadows before. But in place of all this, there is the calm testimony of a good conscience, the citation of the manly soul nerving its noblest powers for duty, the tumultuous rapture of those powers in highest action, the generous action, the generous emulation, the hope of triumph, the joy of victory. And in the midst of this exaltation of soul comes the sudden stroke, and death is finished almost before it is felt. Such an end is not a death; it is a translation. Shall the bereaved count it no consolation? There is proud triumph in it. And it is a triumph not unworthy of a Christian heart. It is even more appropriate to us, than it was to the Greek, to sing

> "Glorious his fate, and envied is his lot,
> Who for his country fights, and for it dies."

For we contend not only for the lawful interests of home and country, but for the more precious and sacred cause of God, and of souls.

Robert L. Dabney, D.D., "The Christian Soldier: A Sermon Commemorative of the Death of Abram C. Carrington," Preached and Published by Order of the Session of College Church, December 1862 (Richmond, Va.: Presbyterian Committee of Publication, 1863), 9–10.

25

DOMESTIC SLAVERY AND THE
CONFEDERATE CAUSE

*White southerners often called female slaves who nursed and raised
the children of wealthy families "Mammy." As the dialogue in this
poem suggests, slaveholding families sometimes viewed such women
in affectionate but still condescending terms.*

"A Southern Scene from Life"

"O, Mammy, have you heard the news?"
Thus spoke a Southern child,
As in her nurse's aged face
She upward glanced and smiled.
"What news you mean, my little one?
It mus' be mighty fine,
To make my darlin's cheek so red,
Her merry blue eyes shine."

"Why, ABRAM LINCOLN—he, you know,
The Yankee President,
Whose ugly picture once we saw,
When up to town we went;
Well, he is going to free you all,
And make you rich and grand,
And you'll be dressed in silks and gold,
Like the proudest in the land.

"A gilded coach shall carry you
Whene'er you wish to ride,

And, Mammy . . . all your work shall be
Forever laid aside."
The eager speaker paused for breath—
And then the old nurse said,
While closer to her swarthy cheek
She pressed the golden head—

"My little Missis stop an' rest,
You's talkin' mighty fas,'
Jist look up dar and tell me what
You sees in yonder glass?
You see old Mammy's wrinkly face
As black as any coal,
An' underneath her hankercher,
Whole heaps of knotty wool.

"My baby's face is white an' red,
Her skin is soft an' fine,
An' on her pretty little head
The yaller ringlets shine;
My chile, who makes dis diff'rence
'Twixt Mammy and 'twixt you?
You reads dear Lord's blessed Book,
An' you kin tell me true.

"De good God says it mus' be so,
An' honey, I, for one,
Wid tankful heart will always say
His holy will be done!
I tanks Mass' LINKIN all de same,
But when I wants for free,
I'll ask de Lord for Glory,
Not poor *buckera* like he.

"An' as for gilded carriages,
Dey's nothing t'all to see,
My Marster's coach dat carries him

Is good enough for me;
An' honey, when your Mammy wants
To change her homespun dress,
She'll pray, like dear, ole Missis,
To be 'clothed wid righteousness.'

My work's been done dis many a day,
An' now I takes my ease,
A-waitin' for de Marser's call,
Jest when ole Marster please;
An' when, at last, de time's done come,
An' poor ole Mammy dies,
Your own dear mother's soft, white hand
Shall close dese tired eyes.

"De dear Lord Jesus soon will call
Old Mammy home to him,
An' he kin wash her guilty soul
From every spot of sin;
An' at His feet I shill sit down,
Who died an' rose for me,
An' den' an' not *till* den, my chile,
Your Mammy will be free.

"My chile, dey say when monkey's clime,
Dey always show dere tails,
And dis ole monkey better had
Staid splittin' of his rails.
Come, little Missis, say your *prayers,*
Let ole Marse LINKIN 'lone,
De Debbil knows who b'longs to him,
An' he'll take care of his own."

"The Bohemian," in *War Songs of the South,* ed. [William Shepperson] (Richmond: West and Johnston, 1862), 180–82.

26

THE AMAZING ESCAPE OF ROBERT SMALLS,
A SLAVE AND STEAMBOAT PILOT

In 1814, William Wells Brown was born in Lexington, Kentucky, the son of a slave mother and a white father. He escaped from slavery at age twenty and worked as an abolitionist lecturer and author. He is best known for his novel Clotel *(1853), the first published novel by an African American. In this passage, Brown tells the story of Robert Smalls, a slave chosen by whites to steer a Confederate transport ship through the harbor at Charleston. Confederate officers trusted him so much that they spent the night on shore in May 1862, leaving the boat in Smalls's hands. Seizing the opportunity, Smalls led an escape that grabbed public attention in the North. In this passage, Brown consistently misspelled Smalls's name, referring to him as "Small."*

At the breaking out of the rebellion, Robert Small was a slave in Charleston, S. C. He stood amid a group of his fellow-slaves, as the soldiers were getting ready to make the assault upon Fort Sumter, and he said to his associates, "This, boys, is the dawn of freedom for our race." Robert, at this time, was employed as a pilot on board the steamboat "Planter," owned at Charleston, and then lying at her dock. The following day, the steamer commenced undergoing alterations necessary to fit her for a gunboat. Robert, when within hearing of the whites, was loud in his talk of what "we'll do with the Yankees, when this boat is ready for sea." The Planter was soon transmogrified into a rebel man-of-war, to be used in and about the rivers and bays near Charleston, and Robert Small was her acknowledged pilot. One of Robert's brothers was second engineer, and a cousin to him was the second mate; the remainder of the crew were all slaves, except the white officers. It was the custom of the captain, chief mate, and chief engineer to spend the night with their families in the city, when the steamer was in port, the vessel being left in charge of Robert. The following is the account of the capture of the boat by her black crew, as given by the Port Royal correspondent of the *New York Commercial Advertiser:*—

"The steamer Planter, which was run away from the rebels by her pilot, Robert Small, is a new tug boat employed about Charleston harbor, which was seized by the Confederate government and converted into a gunboat, mounting a rifled gun forward and a siege gun aft. She has been in the habit of running out to sea to reconnoiter, and was, therefore, no unusual appearance near the forts guarding the entrance. Small, the helmsman and pilot, conceived the idea of running away, and plotted with several friends, slaves like him, to take them off.

"On the evening of May 11, her officers left the ship, then at the wharf in Charleston, and went to their homes. Small then took the firemen and assistant engineers, all of whom were slaves, in his confidence, had the fires banked up, and every thing made ready to start by daylight.

"At quarter to four on Saturday morning, the lines which fastened the vessel to the dock were cast off, and the ship quietly glided into the stream. Here the harbor guard hailed the vessel, but Small promptly gave the countersign, and was allowed to pass.

"The vessel now called at a dock a distance below, where the families of the crew came on board.

"When off Fort Sumter, the sentry on the ramparts hailed the boat, and Small sounded the countersign with the whistle—three shrill sounds and one hissing sound. The vessel being known to the officers of the day, no objection was raised, the sentry only singing out, 'blow the d—d Yankees to hell, or bring one of them in.' 'Ay, ay,' was the answer, and every possible effort was made to get below.

"Hardly was the vessel out of range, when Small ran up a white flag, and went to the United States fleet, where he surrendered the vessel. She had on board seven heavy guns for Fort Ripley, a fort now building in Charleston harbor, which were to be taken thither the next morning.

"Small, with the crew and their families,—sixteen persons,—were sent to the flagship at Port Royal, and an officer placed on board the *Planter,* who took her also to Commodore Dupont's vessel. Small is a middle-aged negro, and his features betray nothing of the firmness of character he displayed. He is said to be one of the most skillful pilots of Charleston, and to have a thorough knowledge of all the ports and inlets on the coast of South Carolina."

We give below the official account of the taking and surrender of the boat to the naval authorities.

U.S. STEAMSHIP AUGUSTA, OFF CHARLESTON, May 13, 1862.

Sir:

I have the honor to inform you that the rebel armed steamer *Planter* was brought out to us this morning from Charleston by eight contrabands, and delivered up to the squadron. Five colored women and three children are also on board. She carried one 32-pounder and one 24-pounder howitzer, and has also on board four large guns, which she was engaged in transporting. I send her to Port Royal at once, in order to take advantage of the present good weather. I send Charleston papers of the 12th, and the very intelligent contraband who was in charge will give you the information which he has brought off. I have the honor to request that you will send back, as soon as convenient, the officer and crew sent on board.

. . . She was the armed dispatch and transportation steamer attached to the engineer department at Charleston, under Brigadier General Ripley, whose bark, a short time since, was brought to the blockading fleet by several contrabands. The bringing out of this steamer, under all the circumstances, would have done credit to any one. At four in the morning, in the absence of the captain, who was on shore, she left her wharf close to the government office and headquarters, with the Palmetto and "Confederate" flags flying, and passed the successive forts, saluting, as usual, by blowing the steam whistle. After getting beyond the range of the last gun, they hauled down the rebel flags, and hoisted a white one. The *Onward* was the inside ship of the blockading squadron in the main channel, and was preparing to fire when her commander made out the white flag. The armament of the steamer is a 32-pounder, or pivot, and a fine 24-pound howitzer. She has besides, on her deck, four other guns, one seven inch rifled, which were to be taken, on the morning of the escape, to the new fort in the middle ground. One of the four belonged to Fort Sumter, and had been struck, in the rebel attack, on the muzzle. Robert Small, the intelligent slave, and pilot of the boat, who performed this bold feat so skilfully, informed me of this fact, presuming it would be a matter of interest to us to have possession of this gun. This man, Robert Small, is superior to any who have come into our lines, intelligent as many of them have been. His information has been most interesting, and portions of it of the utmost importance. The steamer is quite a valuable acquisition to the squadron by her good machinery and very light draught. The officer in charge brought her through St. Helena Sound, and by the inland passage down Beaufort River, arriving here at ten last night. On board the steamer, when she left Charleston, were eight men, five women, and three children. I shall continue to employ Small as pilot on board the *Planter,* for inland waters, with which he appears to be very familiar. I do not know whether, in the view of the government, the vessel will be considered a prize; but if so, I respectfully submit to the Department the claims of the man Small and his associates.

Very respectfully, your obedient servant,
S. F. DUPONT
Flag Officer, Commanding, &c.

A bill was at once introduced in Congress to consider the *Planter* a prize, and to award the prize-money to her crew. The *New York Tribune* had the following editorial on the subject:—

"The House of Representatives at Washington, it is to be hoped, will be more than just to their own sense of right, and to their more generous impulses, than to put aside the Senate bill giving the prize-money they have so well earned to the pilot and crew of the steamer *Planter.* Neither House would have done an act unworthy of their dignity had they promptly passed a vote of thanks to Robert Small and his fellows for the cool courage with which they planned and executed their escape from rebel bondage, and the unswerving loyalty which prompted them, at the same time, to bring away such spoils from the enemy as would make a welcome addition to the blockading squadron.

"If we must still remember with humiliation that the Confederate flag yet waves where our national colors were first struck, we should be all the more prompt to recognize the merit that has put into our possession the first trophy from Fort Sumter. And the country should feel doubly humbled if there is not magnanimity enough to acknowledge a gallant action, because it was the head of a black man that conceived, and the hand of a black man that executed it. It would be better, indeed, become us to remember that no small share of the naval glory of the war belongs to the race which we have forbidden to fight for us; that one negro has recaptured a vessel from a southern privateer, and another has brought away from under the very guns of the enemy, where no fleet of ours has yet dared to venture, a prize whose possession a commodore thinks worthy to be announced in a special dispatch."

The bill was taken up and passed, and the brave Small and his companions received justice at the hands of the government.

William Wells Brown, "Robert Small," in *The Black Man, His Antecedents, His Genius, and His Achievements* (New York: Thomas Hamilton, 1863), 175–79.

27

CONFEDERATE WOMEN AND UNION TROOPS
IN OCCUPIED NEW ORLEANS

The Union Navy captured New Orleans, the largest city in the Confederacy, in April 1862. Initially, pro-Confederate women taunted and spat on occupying Union soldiers. Some reports even claimed that they dumped their chamber pots on Union troops. In response, Benjamin Butler, the military governor of the city, issued his infamous "woman order." This threat to treat white southern women as prostitutes, who at the time had virtually no legal recourse against rape, became emblematic of increasingly harsh U. S. war policies. Most historians agree that the order was effective in reducing demonstrations of disrespect for Union soldiers.

General Orders No. 28.
HDQRS. DEPARTMENT OF THE GULF.

New Orleans, May 15, 1862.
    As the officers and soldiers of the United States have been subject to repeated insults from the women (calling themselves ladies) of New Orleans in return for the most scrupulous non-interference and courtesy on our part, it is ordered that hereafter when any female shall by word, gesture, or movement, insult or show contempt for any officer or soldier of the United States she shall be regarded and held liable to be treated as a woman of the town plying her avocation.

By command of Major General Butler:
GEO. C. STRONG,
Assistant Adjutant-General and Chief of Staff.

The War of the Rebellion: A Compilation of the Official Records of the Union and Confederate Armies (Washington, D.C.: Government Printing Office, 1880–1901), series 1, vol. 15, 426.

28

A SLAVE'S "FAITHFULNESS AND DEVOTION"

This unsigned article describes an astonishingly loyal slave. Such stories were rare even in the Confederate press. Aspects of the account, such as the ease with which "Nathan" passes from one army to another, make the story seem unlikely. However, it provides a glimpse at what Confederate readers desperately wished to believe. To deflect charges of racism, today's admirers of the white southern cause, or "neo-Confederates," have tried to show that many slaves voluntarily fought for the Confederacy. Historians have found no persuasive evidence in support of this contention.

A soldier from the battlefield of Richmond has related the following incident to us, showing the fidelity of the slave to his master. It is worthy of record.

In the fight of Tuesday, near Richmond, a negro man named Nathan, belonging to Lieutenant Williams of Company G, First Georgia Regulars, was captured by a Yankee and taken to the Yankee camp. On Saturday morning the negro was sent to the spring to procure some water for his new master, but instead of performing that task, he kept on his way to Confederate lines, where, on his arrival, at 9 A.M., he presented himself to Gen. Hill to gather with two horses which he captured on his "masterly retreat." The horses were wounded, and General Hill gave them to the negro. Nathan immediately sold one of his horses for $50, but persistently refused to sell the other. He then reported himself to his master, Lieutenant Williams, and is now serving him as faithfully as ever.

The negroes at the South are far too shrewd to be caught by the

Yankees' false promises of freedom, and the present instance is but one of many evidences of their faithfulness and devotion to their masters.

Augusta Constitutionalist, reprinted in the *Charleston Courier,* July 31, 1862.

29

UNION OCCUPATION AND PLANTATION LABOR
IN THE MISSISSIPPI VALLEY

As the Union Army gained ground in Louisiana, officers developed strategies for controlling the labor of African Americans. Some in the War Department, such as General Benjamin Butler, wished for tight control over black labor. While the slave's legal status remained ambiguous, they were effectively free, worked for wages, and produced badly needed cotton. Others hoped to recruit blacks as Union soldiers. As the Union consolidated its hold on New Orleans, Confederates gloated over the Union's difficulties in managing the work of their newfound labor force.

The *New Orleans Bee* has the following:

About 1 o'clock, yesterday morning, the third district was the scene of one of the most desperate negro affairs which the city has ever witnessed. Shortly before that hour the Police of that district discovered coming along the levee a large band of negroes, evidently runaways, and determined to carry out their scheme at all hazards and costs. They were armed with all sorts of weapons which plantations afford, from cane billhooks to clubs.

When they reached Montegut Street, the Police ordered them to halt, and proceeded to arrest them. Instead of surrendering themselves, however, they immediately attacked the Police in a most furious manner. So furious were the negroes that they [the police] were in danger of becoming completely overcome. Their clubs and pistols were freely used, but so numerous was the gang of negroes that they were not equal to the task which had fallen on them . . . assistance from other quarters being absolutely necessary to save the Police a detachment of militia from adjacent quarters hastened to the spot and lent their aid. It did not take long after this to convince the negroes that they were overpowered, for three of them were soon killed, a number desperately wounded, and the mass of them scattered.

The total number of the band, it would seem, was something like 150; but they were not all together at the time of the Police accessing them. They had run off last night from plantations down the coast. From one, that of Thomas Morgan, Esq., some thirty have run off, thirteen of whom are now in the parish prison, nine in the charity hospital, and one killed. Besides the three killed and the nine wounded negroes above noticed, there are others more or less hurt. Four of the police officers, we regret to learn, are pretty badly injured. The affair has created great excitation throughout the city, especially in the lower districts; but is nothing in comparison to what exists in the country below. Apprehensions of the gravest character are felt on all the plantations, and measures for protection against the dreadful evils are being most anxiously canvassed.

Hinds County [Miss.] Gazette, September 3, 1862.

1863

—— 30 ——

A CIVILIAN ON THE DEATH OF A SOLDIER

Joseph Waddell lived in Virginia's Shenandoah Valley. Middle-aged when the war broke out, he worked for the Confederate Quartermaster Department, which supplied food and other goods to the military. A religious man, he believed that God shaped human events. Although events tested his faith, he never wavered in his support of slavery and the Confederacy. However, Waddell expressed deep regret at the conflict's human costs. Here he discussed the death of his nephew, Addy Stuart.

Sunday night, January 4, 1863.

Returning from the cemetery this morning, Va and I walked over the hill and through the ground where deceased soldiers are buried. The number of graves has greatly increased since I was there last. It was almost appalling to see the rows of graves recently dug, waiting with gaping mouths for still living victims. The sight brought before us visibly the sufferings of the soldiers dying in military hospitals, far from home and kindred and all the horrors of a time of war. The small pox cases are buried elsewhere.

Monday night, January 12, 1863.

We have been in deep affliction. At [last] this war has taken a victim from our family. On Thursday, the 8th, I received a dispatch from Mr. Stuart, stating that Addy was dead, that his remains would be brought to Staunton, and requesting me to meet Sister in Lynchburg on Friday. I felt that I had received a staggering blow, and oh! the overwhelming sympathy for his heart-broken mother—he her only son.—And such a son!—So obedient, affectionate, sympathizing—so upright, truthful, and brave. Before he was quite seventeen years of age he entered the army as an "orderly" to Col. Harry L. Edmundson of Roanoke Co. The schools had been disbanded and he was left unemployed and without an associate, all the youths of Christiansburg about his age, being in the service. He became so restless and unhappy, that when the comparatively safe and easy position alluded to was offered to him, his parents allowed him to accept it. He went through the Kentucky campaign, returned to Wytheville, Va., went thence with his regiment to Richmond, and soon afterwards to Petersburg. From every point he wrote to his mother, cheering her up, and assuring her that he would be happy if he only knew she was not in trouble about him. Again he wrote that the regiment was on the point of moving, he knew not wither—next, only four days afterwards, came a dispatch saying that he had died of pneumonia, after an illness of twenty-four hours, and his remains would be forwarded. I met his mother at a hotel in Lynchburg. Friday night, and returned with her to Staunton on Saturday—a most mournful journey. Never can I forget that night as we sat in a dark room, she talking about her loved and loving boy, and I trying to comfort her. Mary, who came to Lynchburg with her mother, returned home next morning in the three o'clock train. And there we sat in the dark, till she shivered with cold, and I persuaded her to lie down. He was a son to love and be proud of. He was cheerful, social, accommodating, conscientious and a universal favorite. Long ago, he came forward, of his own accord; and made a profession of religion—recently, when about to march, he wrote to his mother, "I go cheerfully, trusting in God." We have learned by telegraph to-day that in his last moments his mind was unclouded and hopeful. He died at Franklin, N.C., on Blackwater River. He was a universal favorite, for he was always ready to do a kind act, to whoever needed it. His battalion was dismounted on a recent occasion and required to march on foot, owing to his position he was permitted to retain his horse, but he tendered it to a soldier who, he thought, was less able to walk than himself. All his acquaintances, of every rank, have testified to his noble traits, and expressed affection for him. But he is gone from us—God has ordered it so, and oh let us bow to His will. His stricken mother broke forth into praise when she received the dispatch this morning, stating that in his last moments his mind was unclouded and hopeful. Notwithstanding the arrangements I had made in Lynchburg, the remains passed through that place and went to Christiansburg. They will arrive here to-morrow evening. It is painful to me to write these lines, but I want to have some tribute to the dear boy.—God grant that we all may have true faith in Christ and obedience to Him, so that we shall at last meet in heaven. Mr. Stuart is at home, sick.

"Diary of Joseph Addison Waddell, January 4–12," Online Valley of the Shadow Project, University of Virginia.

31

ANTI-SEMITISM IN THE CONFEDERACY

In 1861 there were only about twenty-five thousand Jews in the Confederate states, most of them recent immigrants of modest means. Still, anti-Semitic rhetoric was pervasive in American culture, and this was reflected in Confederate political discussion.

THE JEWS AND THE WAR.
To the Editor of the Richmond Examiner:

Among the prevailing fashions, none perhaps has grasped the public mind with a firmer hold, and none withal is fraught at times with more cruel injustice than that of seeking in a particular individual or a separate class scapegoats for the general disappointment at failures or indignation at crimes. . . . But the practice now generally obtaining of ascribing the faults of a whole community to a particular class or the kindred error of condemning a race for the conduct of individuals is so unjust, ungenerous, and unfair, that it behooves those who see its injustice to cry out in earnest protest against it, so all Babeldom should clamour in consequence.

Conspicuous among the examples of this conduct is the indiscriminate and perpetual assault upon our fellow citizens of the Hebrew faith. . . .

It is asserted that they have not furnished their quota of men for the public defence. To the extent that this charge is well founded, and it is not true to the extent that it applies to other classes of our people, it is attributable mainly to two causes. In the first place, our Jewish fellow-citizens rarely mix in politics, either in its toils or its gains. . . . Trade (and the Jews are all tradesmen) is proverbially conservative, peaceful, timid. The fighting of the world in all battles for freedom has been done by the farmers and the gentry, the artizan and the professional man. Moreover, to the considerations which impel all men to avoid the perils of war, there is added, in the case of the man of trade, the extraordinary inducement of the unexampled profits of which a time of civil disorder furnishes the occasion, the temptation and the means. Let us look around among our Gentile trade community, and ask ourselves if the same feverish anxiety to obtain an exemption, or "put in a substitute," is not the prevailing character of all? Which conduct is more reprehensible, that of the Jews, who have remained in their old channels of business, enlarging and extending them, or that of those Gentiles who, from every profession and pursuit, from that of the clergyman to the seller of "truck," have rushed into the wildest speculations? When many of the latter were among the most blatant of our secession friends, the Jews have still less reason to shrink from the comparison.

. . . The other charge is that of "infamous extortion." If extortion means buying as cheaply as possible and selling it dearly, I know one Gentile firm in Charleston that has profited more by extortion than all the Jews on Broad Street, and I fancy that a woolen firm in Richmond or a certain flouring establishment or a certain foundry might run a similar race with considerable prospects of success. Those who make the charge in turn to the great cotton factories, to the Iron factories, to the tanneries, to the commission houses, to the railroad companies, to the importers, to every conceivable branch of business; but especially to the vast storehouse of villainous corruption and fast profits in which, as in all I have named above, Christians enjoy an undivided monopoly of extortion.

If, finally, it be true that many of our Jewish fellow-citizens have accumulated fortunes in the progress of this unhappy war, it is no less true that among those who have given of their abundance with lavish hand to every enterprise having the benefit of the soldier for its object, a conspicuous place may be claimed for the men and women of that faith. . . .

Such, Mr. Editor, are the candid sentiments of a volunteer, "who does not sign himself *Moses,*" and is NOT A JEW.

Petersburg, December 22, 1862, in the *Charleston Mercury,* January 9, 1863.

32

A BREAD RIOT IN RICHMOND
(FOUR DOCUMENTS)

*By 1862, famished women on the home front suffered from high prices
driven by runaway inflation. In their view, merchants and shopkeepers
violated traditional ideas of economic fairness and undermined the
southern cause.*

"Extortion and the Extortioners"
"The love of money is the root of evil."—Paul

The temptation to become suddenly rich is too strong for thousands of people. Money is a good thing, but the LOVE *of money* is the
root of evil, and a snare of the Devil by which thousands have been
entrapped, and hurried to perdition. It is a bad condition of society
when a spirit of gainful speculation possesses all ranks of the people,
from the urchin, who sharply turns a penny in a goose quill speculation, to the landed lordling whose conscience is sealed up by the lust
for gain. The most painful feature of the times is, the unrighteous
and wholesale extortion, which is practiced upon the government and
upon the people—especially on that portion of the people, which is
now in the field to defend the lives and property of the greedy land-
sharks who are seeking to eat out the subsistence of the country.

The whole trading community seems to have lost its reason, become
money-mad, and there is a great danger, from the signs, that the whole
of the stay-at-home community will become traders and thus to be
effectively *Yankeeized,* as if they had been "brought up" in the land of
wooden nutmegs. The thing is really contagious, and men have been,
and are, afflicted with the disease who, when sober reason resumes

her empire, will be astonished and mortified at their weakness, but the plague-spot will never leave their hands, as it has been burnt in too deeply by extortionate gain. *Self-respect* is worth more than gold!

There is extortion on every hand; the most bare-faced and unjustifiable extortion is practiced upon the poor soldiers in the camps by those whose very property the soldiers are protecting from the incursions of the enemy. Mr. All-gain immediately shows his self-serving patriotism, and approbation of the noble volunteers, by supplying them with apples from his extensive orchard at the moderate charge of ten cents each! No fiction this.

We have every-thing to fear from this reckless spirit of gain, this unholy extortion. The Church will be ruined by it, the State will be ruined by it, the social system will be ruined by it. The god Mammon will become the god of the people, and on his altar every honorable impulse, every noble instinct of humanity, will be sacrificed. We had as well be under Yankee rule as under the rule of the heartless monster.

EDITOR
Camp near Evansport [Virginia]

Christian Intelligencer [Richmond, Virginia], January 25, 1863.

In 1863, Confederate women, many of whom described themselves as soldiers' wives, began protesting and rioting against wartime shortages, especially of food. While crowd actions in Richmond, the Confederate capitol, received the most attention, similar demonstrations occurred in Georgia and North Carolina. John B. Jones, a clerk in the War Department, observed the Richmond bread riot from his vantage point in the center of the city.

APRIL 2d. [1863]
This morning early a few hundred women and boys met as by concert in the Capitol Square, saying they were hungry, and must have food. The number continued to swell until there were more

than a thousand. But few men were among them, and these were mostly foreign residents, with exemptions in their pockets. About nine A.M. the mob emerged from the western gates of the square, and proceeded down Ninth Street, passing the War Department, and crossing Main Street, increasing in magnitude at every step, but preserving silence and (so far) good order. Not knowing the meaning of such a procession, I asked a pale boy where they were going. A young woman, seemingly emaciated, but yet with a smile, answered that they were going to find something to eat. I could not, for the life of me, refrain from expressing the hope that they might be successful; and I remarked they were going in the right direction to find plenty in the hands of the extortioners. I did not follow, to see what they did; but I learned an hour after that they marched through Cary Street, and entered diverse stores of the speculators, which they proceeded to empty of their contents. They impressed all the carts and drays in the street, which were speedily laden with meal, flour, shoes, etc. I did not learn whither these were driven; but probably they were rescued from those in charge of them. Nevertheless, an immense amount of provisions, and other articles, were borne by the mob, which continued to increase in numbers. An eye-witness says he saw a boy come out of a store with a hat full of money (notes); and I learned that when the mob turned up into Main Street, when all the shops were by this time closed, they broke in the plate-glass windows, demanding silks, jewelry, etc. Here they were incited to pillage valuables, not necessary for subsistence, by the class of residents (aliens) exempted from military duty by Judge [John Archibald] Campbell, Assistant Secretary of War, in contravention of Judge Meredith's decision. Thus the work of spoliation went on, until the military appeared upon the scene, summoned by Gov. [John] Letcher, whose term of service is near its close. He had the Riot Act read (by the mayor), and then threatened to fire on the mob. He gave them five minutes' time to disperse in, threatening to use military force (the city battalion being present) if they did not comply with the demand. The timid women fell back, and a pause was put to the devastation, though but few believed he would venture to put his threat in execution. If he had done so, he would have been hung, no doubt.

About this time the President appeared, and ascending a dray, spoke to the people. He urged them to return to their homes, so that the bayonets there menacing them might be sent against the common enemy. He told them that such acts would bring *famine* upon them in the only form which could not be provided against, as it would deter people from bringing food to the city. He said he was willing to share his last loaf with the suffering people (his best horse had been stolen the night before), and he trusted we would all bear our privations with fortitude, and continue united against the Northern invaders, who were the authors of all our sufferings. He seemed deeply moved; and indeed it was a frightful spectacle, and perhaps an ominous one, if the government does not remove some of the quartermasters who have contributed very much to bring about the evil of scarcity. I mean those who have allowed transportation to forestallers and extortioners.

Gen. [Arnold] Elzey and Gen. [John Henry] Winder waited upon the Secretary of War in the morning, asking permission to call the troops from the camps near the city, to suppress the women and children by a summary process. But Mr. [James] Seddon hesitated, and then declined authorizing any such absurdity. He said it was a municipal or State duty, and therefore he would not take the responsibility of interfering in the matter. Even in the moment of aspen consternation, he was still the politician.

I have not heard of any injuries sustained by the women and children. Nor have I heard how many stores the mob visited; and it must have been many.

All is quiet now (three P.M.); and I understand the government is issuing rice to the people.

John B. Jones, *A Rebel War Clerk's Diary* (Philadelphia: Lippincott, 1866), 284–87.

The Richmond Sentinel *initially tried to suppress news of the bread riot. When news of the riot became public, it condemned the women who had participated in the it.*

When the public peace was, for a time, somewhat disturbed here, on Thursday last, it was suggested to us and the rest of the city press, by many citizens, to refrain from any present notice of it, on account of the misrepresentations and exaggerations to which a publication would give rise. In assenting to this suggestion, in company with all the other papers, we felt that we were only paying a decent respect to the opinions of gentleman certainly as well qualified to judge as ourselves, equally interested, to say the least, in a correct judgment, and entitled to deference on other grounds. Our compliance was voluntary and in good faith. We thus became a party to the reserve. We have no repentance for this, nor have we any quarrel, or any reproaches where our hand has been given. We have not even any regrets. On the contrary, we are glad that time was taken to ascertain facts with precision, and thus to prevent errors which a precipitate notice might have assisted to spread.

It can now be said, upon the authority of the sworn evidence, that the conduct of a few misguided women who on Thursday availed of the tenderness with which their sex is ever treated in the South, was not due to suffering. They and the thieves in pantaloons who took shelter in their company, simply plundered milliners' goods, dry goods, fancy foods, &c. It was no cry for Bread; it was no riot, so far as they placed their action on any declared basis. It was opposition to the high prices; and upon this point they took shelter under the abstract sympathy of such as believed that speculators and extortioners have made the prices so high, and dispose them accordingly.

But it is now proven that there was no distress among these persons; that the very leader was independent, and himself an extortioner; that there has been abundant provision made for the poor who may need it and that the whole thing was simply a plundering raid under female impunity. An ebullition such as we have noticed would have excited no attention outside of the quiet South, where good order is so uniform and so universal.

Richmond Sentinel, April 7, 1863.

The daughter of a Baptist minister, Sara Agnes Rice Pryor grew up in Charlottesville, Virginia. During the war she worked in Richmond as a nurse. While Pryor's memoir is based on her own experiences, she attributes authorship of this letter describing the bread riot to a friend.

[April 4, 1863]

"Yesterday, upon arriving [at the Capitol Square] I found within the gates a crowd of women and boys—several hundreds of them, standing quietly together. I sat on a bench near, and one of the number left the rest then took the seat beside me. She was a pale, emaciated girl, not more than eighteen, with a sunbonnet on her head, and dressed in a clean calico gown. 'I could stand it no longer,' she exclaimed. As I made room for her, I observed that she had delicate features and large gloves. As she raised her hand to remove her sunbonnet and use it for a fan, her loose calico sleeve slipped up, and revealed a mere skeleton of an arm. She perceived my expression as I looked at it, and hastily pulled down her sleeve with a short laugh. 'This is all that's left of me!' she said. 'It seems real funny don't it?' Evidently, she had been a pretty girl—a dressmaker's apprentice, I judged from her chafed forefinger and a certain skill in the lines of her gown. I was encouraged to ask: 'What is it? Is there some celebration?'

"'There is,' said the girl, solemnly, 'we celebrate our right to live. We are starving. As soon as enough of us get together we are going to the bakeries and each of us will take a loaf of bread. That is little enough for the government to give us after it has taken all our men.'

"Just then a fat old black Mammy waddled up the walk to overtake a beautiful child who was running before her. 'Come dis a way, honey, she called, 'don't go nigh dem people,' adding, in a lower tone, 'I's feared you'll ketch something' fum dem white folks. I wonder dey lets 'em in de Park.'

"The girl turned to me with a wan smile, as she rose to join the long line that now formed and was moving, she said simply, 'Goodbye! I'm going to get something to eat!'

"'And I devoutly hope you'll get it—and plenty of it,' I told her.

"The crowd now rapidly increased, and numbered, I am sure, more than a thousand women and children. It grew and grew until it reached the dignity of a mob—a bread riot. They impressed all the light carts they met, and marched along silently and in order. They marched through Cary Street and Main, visiting the stores of speculators and emptying them of their contents. Governor Letcher sent the Mayor to read the Riot Act, and as this had no effect he threatened to fire on the crowd. The city battalion came up. The women fell back with frightened eyes, but did not obey the order to disperse. The President then appeared, ascended a dray, and addressed them. It is said that he was received at first with hisses from the boys, but after he had spoken some little time with great kindness and sympathy, the women quietly moved on, taking their food with them. General Elzey and General Winder wished to call troops from the camp to 'suppress the women,' but Mr. Seddon, wise man, declined to issue the order. While I write women and children are still standing in the streets, demanding food, and the government is issuing them rations of rice."

Sara Agnes Rice Pryor, *Reminiscences of Peace and War* (New York: Macmillan, 1905), 238.

—— 33 ——

A LOUISIANA WOMAN DESCRIBES THE ARRIVAL OF UNION TROOPS

Kate Stone's journal, quoted earlier, continued her remarkably eloquent story of refugee life. In this passage she describes her terror when Union troops, most of them African American, arrive at her family's plantation.

Near Trenton, La. *April 25* [1863]:

We walked in and found Mrs. Hardison and the children all much excited and very angry, with flaming cheeks and flashing eyes. The Negroes had been very impertinent. The first armed Negroes they had ever seen. Just as we were seated someone called out the Yankees were coming again. It was too late to run. All we could do was to shut ourselves up together in one room, hoping they would not come in. George Richards was on the gallery. In a minute we heard the gate open and shut, rough hoarse voices, a volley of oaths, and then a cry, "Shoot him, curse him! Shoot him! Get out of the way so I can get him." Looking out of the window, we saw three fiendish-looking black Negroes standing around George Richards, two with their guns leveled and almost touching his breast. He was deathly pale but did not move. We thought he would be killed instantly, and I shut my eyes that I might not see it. But after a few words from George, which we could not hear, and another volley of curses, they lowered their guns and rushed into the house "to look for guns" they said, but only to rob and terrorize us. The Negroes were completely armed and there was no white man with them. We heard them ranging all through the house, cursing and laughing, and breaking things open.

Directly one came bursting into our room, a big black wretch, with the most insolent swagger, talking all the time in a most insulting manner. He went through all the drawers and wardrobe taking anything he fancied, all the time with a cocked pistol in his hand. Cursing and making the most awful threats against Mr. Hardison if they ever caught him, he lunged up to the bed where the baby was sleeping. Raising the bar, he started to take the child, [the Hardison's baby], saying as he waved the pistol, "I ought to kill him. He may grow up to be a jarilla [guerrilla]. Kill him." Mrs. Hardison sprang to his side, snatched the baby up, and shrieked, "Don't kill my baby. Don't kill him." The Negro turned away with a laugh and came over where I was sitting with Little Sister crouched close to me holding my hand. He came right up to us standing on the hem of my dress while he looked me slowly over, gesticulating and snapping his pistol. He stood there about a minute, I suppose. It seemed to me an age. I felt like I would die should he touch me. I did not look up or move, and Little Sister was as still as if petrified. In an instant more he turned away with a most diabolical laugh, gathered up his plunder, and went out. I was never so frightened in my life. Mrs. Hardison said we were both [Kate and Little Sister] as white as marble, and she was sure I would faint. What a wave of thankfulness swept over us when he went out and slammed the door. In the meanwhile, the other Negroes were rummaging the house, ransacking it from top to bottom, destroying all the provisions they could not carry away, and sprinkling a white powder into the cisterns and over everything they left. We never knew whether it was poison or not.

The Negroes called and stormed and cursed through the house, calling each other "Captain" and "Lieutenant" until it nearly froze the blood in our veins, and every minute we expected them to break into our room again. I was completely unnerved. I did not think I could feel so frightened.

Kate Stone's family lost most of their property. Still, her account of their flight from Union troops emphasized the family's good fortune in surviving the ordeal.

[Near Trenton, La.] *April 27* [1863]

Mamma and Johnny are out hunting up bed clothes and anything else buyable since we need everything, and Sister and I are left to ourselves this rainy day. So I may as well finish the recital of our woes.

We left our clothes in care of Uncle Bob who has been as faithful as any white man could be. He is Mamma's driver on the plantation. And we piled ourselves and our scanty luggage into two rocking, leaky dugouts and pushed off, Jimmy paddling one and Coffee, one of Dr. Carson's hands, the other. The sight of a body of horsemen in the distance coming our way lent strength to their arms, and as fast as they could ply the paddles we glided through the water. The men came on down the road, and we saw they were Yankee soldiers. But the water was so deep that they could not ride fast and we kept ahead At last after nearly a mile of this race, the boats shot out into deep water, and we were safe from pursuit. Then what a shout rang out for Jeff Davis and the Confederacy. The men could see and hear us distinctly, and we half expected a volley to come whizzing over the waters. But the boys would not be restrained, and their "Farewell to the Feds!" "Hurrah for Jeff Davis!" and "Ho for Texas!" floated over the waters till we were out of sight. The Yankees followed us until their horses were nearly swimming.

After rowing a few miles, we joined Mr. Hardison and his family at the Jones place in the middle of Tensas swamp. They were in a skiff and had been waiting for us for some time. All his family and all his worldly possessions were in that skiff and it was not loaded, so quickly had he been reduced from affluence to poverty. We went on in company and were in the boats for seven hours in the beating rain and the sickening sun, sitting with our feet in the water. Not an inch of land was to be seen during the journey through the dense swamp over the swift curling currents. The water was sometimes twenty feet deep, rushing and gurgling around the logs and trees. We all stood it very well except Aunt Laura. She was terrified nearly to death and was alternately laughing and crying. She insisted on giving the rower directions and, as he was a slow African, confused him so that he forgot how to pull and ran us into brush piles innumerable. At last he said, "Now, Mistress, you just tell me how to pull and I'll do it." So Aunt Laura and Mamma steered the boat *viva voce,* and he did the hard pulling. I thought they surely would make him turn us over, since a dugout goes over with such ease. At last we came to a clearing, and the boats had to be pulled over the land. We walked a path lined with brambles, and our dresses were nearly torn off. Johnny suffered with fever nearly all day.

When Stone's family reached safety in Texas, they faced social isolation in an insular community.

[Tyler, Tex.] *Nov. 1* [1863]

We are just from church. Jimmy, Johnny, and I did not go *con amore.* There are more pleasant things than toiling a mile through heavy sand, up hill and down dale—too dark to see the road beneath you or the sky above, sitting for an hour listening to an indifferent sermon, and being gazed at by a battery of hostile eyes. Jimmy was determined to go and I would go too, though he did not want me. Last night he and Johnny went alone, and during the services someone cut his bridle all to pieces and stole his martingale and blanket. A crowd of boys followed them after church, talking at them all the time. They know now the boys are armed and so did not attack them. The rowdies followed us tonight and I saw them for the first time. They are real nice-looking lads. What a pity they are not gentlemen. Jimmy Carson is deeply mortified that he is compelled to desert a friend in need.

[Tyler, Tex.] *Jan. 4* [1864]

We were glad to see the Old Year go. It had been a year of trial to us, and we rejoiced when we caught the last glimpse of the sail bearing him on to the dim Ocean of Eternity. The New Year came wailing in, borne on the wings of the freezing norther. God grant it may bring peace to our warworn land and those we love home again.

Mrs. Savage and her cortège, with Dr. Meagher in the train, arrived Tuesday and are busy settling in their new quarters. The little girls have been staying in here with us until today. We found five in the room with insufficient bedclothes rather too much for comfort in this freezing weather. I very foolishly allowed myself to be persuaded to spend the first night out in camp with them, and I have not recovered from it yet. I feel like blushing every time I think of it as we all practically slept together with only a curtain separating the tent into two rooms and the mattresses touching each other. I never felt so out of place. Anna is the same as ever, but Emily Norris has outgrown the name of little girl. She has developed very rapidly and promises to be a noted flirt.

John Q. Anderson, ed., *Brokenburn: The Journal of Kate Stone, 1861–1868* (Baton Rouge: Louisiana State Univ. Press, 1955), 195–96, 200–202, 252, 272.

34

THE CONFEDERATE PUBLIC MOURNS A HERO

Confederate general Thomas "Stonewall" Jackson was known and loved not only for his military success, but also for his conspicuous religious faith and military brilliance. His death in May 1863 caused an outpouring of public grief. Jackson taught at the Virginia Military Institute (VMI) in the 1850s, and was by all accounts a poor classroom instructor. However, his military success earned him the heartfelt admiration of VMI cadets. Cadet Samuel B. Hannah described the scene at the Institute at the time of Jackson's death.

VMI Institute
May 17, 1863.

I was Officer of the Day when the body of Gen. Jackson was brought in Barracks: no military escort accompanied him from Richmond, only a few citizens, among them the Gov. His body was said to be embalmed, but of no avail. Decomposition had already taken place, in consequence of which his face was not exposed to view as the features were said not to be natural. The coffin was a perfect flower bed and under that, which was presented to his wife by the President, the first new Confederate flag ever made. His body was placed in his old Section room which will remain draped for six months.

Gen. [Francis] Smith then requested that none of the flowers should be removed from the coffin which was an impossibility although I had a Sentinel posted over the remains. Still the Sentinels would remove things for themselves and of course they were afraid to inform on others for fear of being caught at it themselves. I did not think in right to take what others had placed there as a memorial of their love and esteem for our beloved Jackson, although I would prize a trophy like that the highest imaginable. Still as it had been entrusted to me to see that all was kept right, so long as his body was under my charge I couldn't conscientiously take any of the flowers when I knew that every cadet was afraid to let me see him take or touch the body.

He only remained in Barracks one day and night. He was buried on Friday the 15th of May. Dr [William] White preached his funeral, the old Gentleman seemed and I know he was deeply afflicted, for from all accounts the Gen. took quite an active part in the church and was the founder of the Colored Sunday School and the main stay of it as long as he was in Lexington.

Cadet Samuel P. Hannah to an unknown recipient, May 17, 1863, Preston Library, Virginia Military Institute.

35

THE MYSTERIOUS DEATH OF A SLAVE WOMAN

Emma Holmes, the daughter of a rich slaveholder, passed most of the war in Camden, South Carolina. This intelligent young woman seems extraordinarily naive about the brutality of slavery, especially in her own family.

March 12, 1863

. . . Mother received a letter last night from Carrie, which she had not read to us, & she only seemed so troubled that it affected me & I feared Carrie might have been more sick than she first wrote. But today she told us the dreadful truth. Margaret had become so excessively negligent & indifferent to her duties & withal so impertinent that Carrie asked Isaac to punish her. He, who is always so kind & thoughtful even towards a servant, would not do so during the day so as not to disgrace her before the other servants but took her after dark to an extreme end of the garden, intending to reprimand her & with a light strap gave her two or three cuts across her shoulders. She tore away from him with one wrench, tore off all her clothing, which must have been previously loosened purposely, and to his astonishment sprang into the creek. He called to her to come out, for she stood waist deep, and [then he] stepped behind a tree. Without answering she *plunged head foremost* & he only saw her head rise. He hastened to the house & sent Marcus to assist her & persuade her to come out, but he could find no traces of her. Mr. Bull had the creek dragged unsuccessfully for the wind was high & the current must have swept the body out. Marcus who had taken great interest in her & talked to her to make her behave better then told Isaac that she had told him a few days ago that if she was ever touched again she would drown or kill herself—yet confessed she had plenty to eat & to wear, had little to do, and was kindly treated, as all the servants bore witness. But none dreamed of such a demoniac temper, for as long as we had her about us, often punishing her necessarily in various ways, it had never been shown to any of us.

It put poor Isaac nearly crazy, for he blamed himself as the cause of her suicide, accusing himself of undue severity. Carrie said she hopes never to spend such another awful night—to see a strong man bowed with fearful anguish, weeping like a little child and accusing himself almost as a murderer—[it] was *too terrible*. The first night they hoped she had crept into the marsh & was ashamed to come up in the day without clothes, was probably waiting for night to come back. . . . Carrie was so worried about her, for the weather was cold and bleak. Her body was not found for two or three days, then Isaac had it examined by physicians and other gentlemen to prove that there was no mark of violence, then staid himself to see her buried. But it was too much for him. Again that terrible anguish swept over his soul—that the public might think him the cause of her death. Poor fellow, to have his peace of mind destroyed by the blind rage of such a creature is too dreadful.

Mother told Nina to break it to Judy; the latter took it more calmly than we feared, exculpated Isaac & only blamed her daughter's temper which all the servants knew, but we did not. Nina says her aunt on Washington plantation did *exactly* the same thing when about to be punished by the negro driver, and she was only saved from being drowned by some boats that were passing by. It occasioned [in] her a serious fit of illness, & when I knew her, [she] always appeared to be as good natured as possible. The servants say that among them she showed her temper as rude, rough & headstrong as possible, & as impudent to all, even her mother. But still nothing like this had ever been shown nor would any have ever dreamed it possible. Ann said, "Why missis, that girl had a wicked heart, & my last charge when she went off was to behave herself, and not have Miss Carrie scold her for her carelessness." But ever since she went down she has given a great deal of trouble. We always thought her a rather dull girl, who was hard to teach anything, but that she would go to a beaten track, though we soon found her very careless & slovenly &, though often sullen when scolded or punished, we never saw an outbreak, therefore, never guessed it.

John F. Marszalek, ed., *The Diary of Miss Emma Holmes, 1861–1866* (Baton Rouge: Louisiana State Univ. Press, 1979), 236–38.

RUNAWAY SLAVE ADVERTISEMENTS

These advertisements appeared in a single column in the Rockingham Register, *a newspaper based in Virginia's Shenandoah Valley, on May 29, 1863. Across the South, the presence of the Union armies nearby provided a chance for slaves there to escape, but to seize that opportunity required extraordinary bravery. Slaveholders went to great lengths to chase down and punish, even torture, fugitives. Still, historians estimate that about seven hundred thousand slaves successfully reached Union lines.*

$100 REWARD

Ran away from the subscriber, living on the Shenandoah River in Rockingham County on 29 March, my NEGRO GIRL MARGARET ANN. She is a dark mulatto, 15 years of age, 5 feet, 5 inches high, has a full head of hair, is square shouldered, and has very large feet for a woman. She has a very fierce look, and a little lisp in her talk. She wears a black cloth hat with a purple ribbon on it. She also has a red calico sunbonnet, which of these she wore, I do not know. I will give $100 reward for her return to me, or for her arrest and confinement in any jail, and information of that fact conveyed to me, so that I can get her again.

May 22.
John W. Duvel

*   *   *

$750 REWARD

RAN AWAY from the subscriber, at Buena Vista Furnace, Rockbridge County, on Sunday night last, the 3rd of May, the following THREE NEGRO MEN, all of whom were recently purchased in Richmond, viz.:

SANDY, aged 25 years, 5 foot, 6 inches high, dark color and bright countenance.

JERRY, aged 21 years, 5 feet, 8 ½ inches high, gingerbread color.

BRYANT, 5 feet, 10 ½ inches high, dark mulatto, scar at root of forefinger on right hand.

I have reason to believe they are trying to reach the enemy lying down the Valley. I will give the above reward for the apprehension of all of them, or $200 each for one of them, arrested and put in jail so I can get them, or $250 each for their delivery at my Furnace near Lexington, Rockbridge County, Va.

May 9.
S. P. Jordan

*   *   *

$50 REWARD

Ran away from the subscriber, living near Staunton on Sunday night last, A NEGRO WOMAN AND HER SON, a boy about 3 years of age. The woman is named Sarah, and is a dark mulatto about 22 years of age, about 5 feet four or 5 inches height. Clothing not remembered. Her son is named Aleck and is about the same color as his mother. These negroes belong to the estate of Capt. Powers, dec'd of Loudoun County, are most probably trying to make their way down the Valley to the Yankee lines. The above reward will be paid for the apprehension of the woman and boy out of the county of Augusta; if within the county, $25.

May 22–2t.
J. Wayne Splitler

*   *   *

$75 REWARD—HORSES STOLEN

STOLEN from my pasture field, near Cabin Hill, Shenandoah County, on Sunday night last. A DARK SORREL HORSE and A ROAN MARE.

The horse has a small narrow ball all the way down his face, his mane is pretty much white, and he is branded with the letters, W. and two J's. The mare is nearly 18 hands high, and has three white feet. (The two hind feet and one fore foot). Has a big heavy tail and is branded with the words W. and J. I will pay $75 reward for the horse and mare, or for information by which I may be enabled to get them again. My P. O. is Mt. Clifton, Shenandoah County, Va.

May 22.
JACOB WOLF.

Rockingham Register, May 29, 1863.

37

A CONFEDERATE PARTISAN ON THE AFTERMATH OF BATTLE

James Joseph Williamson served in Mosby's Rangers, a group of Confederate partisans fighting behind Union lines in northern Virginia. Such efforts hindered Union attempts to hold southern territory. In this ghoulish diary entry, Williamson described the human and environmental devastation in the aftermath of battle.

June 21, 1863

During the excitement of a battle one does not so fully realize the terrible effects as when going over the field afterwards. On the morning after the fight (Monday, 22d) white men and negroes were engaged in burying the dead. One poor fellow lay in a fence corner, his brains spattered over the rails, while another had one-half of his head carried away by a shell. Another looked as if calmly sleeping, death had come to him so quickly. In one field, in front of the house at Ayreshire (the residence of Mr. Geo. S. Ayre), where Stuart made a desperate charge to save his train of wagons and ambulances, I counted 31 dead horses. The ground in many places was torn up in great holes and furrows by shot and shell. Roads through the fields in all directions, and big gaps in the stone fences, showed where the cavalry and artillery had ploughed through. The country around presented a scene of desolation; wheat fields trodden down and cornfields in many places looking as though they had never been planted. A poor horse that had one of its hind legs shot away, had grazed around in a circle. I thought it an act of mercy to put a ball through the head of the suffering creature.

A little darkey, looking over the lines into the clover field, saw a fine cavalry boot among the clover and ran to get it, saying in great glee, "Oh, see what a nice boot I've found!" But when he attempted to pick it up and discovered that there was a foot and part of a leg in the boot, he was paralyzed with fright for a few seconds; but he soon recovered the use of his legs and scampered off in a hurry.

James Joseph Williamson, *Mosby's Rangers: A Record of the Operations of the Forty-Third Battalion, Virginia Cavalry, from Its Organization to the Surrender, from the Diary of a Private* (New York: R. B. Kenyon, 1896), 75–76.

38

A CONFEDERATE GOVERNOR ON THE
WAR AT HOME

While he professed loyalty to the Confederacy, Georgia's Governor Joseph Brown was a thorn in the side of Jefferson Davis. He opposed Davis's policy of national conscription, which he argued was unconstitutional. As Federal troops approached his state, he sought to mobilize citizens, including those who had avoided the draft, to save Georgia from the Union armies.

PROCLAMATION
EXECUTIVE DEPARTMENT
Milledgeville Georgia June 22, 1863
Joseph Brown, Governor

To the People of Georgia:

It is not doubted that our enemies are increasing their cavalry force and making preparations to send raids of mounted men through Georgia, as well as other states, to burn all public property in our cities, destroy our railroad bridges, workshops, factories, mills, and provisions, leaving our country, now the home of a happy people, little better than a desolate waste behind them.

They have met our troops in battle and again and again been ingloriously defeated and driven back. Despairing of their ability to conquer us in honorable warfare, they now violate all of the rules of war as recognized by civilized nations, disregard the rights of private property, arm our slaves against us, and send their robber bands among us to plunder, steal and destroy, having no respect even for the rights or the necessities of infirm old age, or of helpless women and children.

To hold in check the mighty hosts collected for our destruction by the Abolition Government, the President is obliged to mass the provisional armies of the Confederacy at a few key points and can not, without weakening them too much, detach troops to defend the interior points against sudden incursions. He therefore calls upon the people of the respective States, who are otherwise not subject to be summoned to the field, under the Conscription Laws of Congress, to organize; and while they attend to their ordinary avocations at home to stand ready at a moment's warning to take up arms and drive back the plundering bands of marauders from their own immediate section of the country.

. . . The Government appreciates the necessity of having the productive labor of the country not subject to conscription as free as possible, to make all the provisions and other supplies of clothing, etc. which can be made, and it is not intended to call this class from their occupations at any time for a longer period than is indispensable to drive the enemies from our midst. Will Georgians refuse to volunteer for this defense? The man able to bear arms who will wait for a draft before he will join an organization to repel the enemy, whose brutal soldiery comes to his home to destroy his property and insult and cruelly injure his wife and his daughters, is unworthy of the proud name of Georgian, and should fear lest he is marked as disloyal to the land of his birth and the government that throws over him the aegis of protection, in case of capture by the enemy, which is enjoyed by other troops in service, including the right to be exchanged as prisoners of war.

Georgians, I appeal to your patriotism and your pride. Let the people of no other State excel you in promptness of action or in the overwhelming numbers tendering in response to the President's call. Your brethren in the field have undergone hardships and endured privations to which you have not been exposed, and have nobly illustrated the character of the State when in deadly conflict with the enemy. The time has now arrived when you are expected to defend their homes and your own in the interior, while they defend the border. Gray-headed sires, your influence and your aid are invoked. The crisis in our affairs is fast approaching. *Georgia expects every man to do his duty.* Fly to arms and trust God to defend the right.

Given under my hand and the seal of the Executive Department, at the Capitol, in Milledgeville, this 23rd Day of June, 1863.

Joseph E. Brown

Albert D. Candler, ed., *Confederate Records of the State of Georgia,* vol. 2 (Atlanta, Ga.: Charles P. Byrd, 1910), 457–62.

39

AN ALABAMA "BELLE" LEAVES HOME

Virginia Clay-Copton was a socialite and the wife of Confederate senator Clement Claiborne Clay. She was a resident of Huntsville, in northern Alabama. Poor transportation left Huntsville isolated from state authorities in Montgomery, but most of the white population remained loyal to the Confederacy.

"We arrived safely (self, Kate, Alice and servants)," I wrote in a kaleidoscopic account which I gave to my husband of the indication of the times as seen *en route* . . . with a single large trunk. Arriving at Chattanooga, we would have been forced to go to the small-pox hotel or remain in the streets but for the gallantry of an acquaintance of ours, an army officer of Washington memory, who gave up his room to us, and furnished some wagons to have our baggage hauled to the depot. At Atlanta there was a scatteration of our forces. . . . When night came" (being fearful of robbery, for hotels were unsafe), "I stuffed in one stocking all my money, and in the other, mine and Alice's watches, chains, pins, and charms. . . . We fumigated the room, had a bed brought for Emily, and retired. At breakfast, Colonel G. G. Garner told me that Uncle Jones [Withers] was in the house, and in a few minutes he presented himself. He got in at three that morning, *en route* for Mobile with thirty days' leave; looked worn, and was sad, I thought. Colonel George Johnson, of Marion, also called, and we had them all and Dr. W., of Macon, to accompany us to the cars. The guard at the gate said 'Passport, Madam,' but I replied, 'Look at my squad; General Withers, Colonel Garner of Bragg's staff, and a Colonel and Lieutenant in the Confederate service. I think I'll *pass!*'" And I passed! . . . Upon his arrival at Richmond, Senator Clay found the conditions such as to render my joining him, if not impracticable, at least inadvisable. The evils of a year agone had multiplied tenfold. Food was growing scarcer; the city's capacity was tested to the uttermost, and lodgings difficult to obtain. The price of board for my husband alone now amounted to more than his income. . . .

Virginia Clay-Copton, *A Belle of the Fifties, Memoirs of Mrs. Clay, of Alabama, Covering Social and Political Life in Washington and the South, 1853–66,* ed. Ada Sterling (New York: Doubleday, Page, and Company, 1904), 192–93.

40

MASTERS AND SLAVES IN
OCCUPIED MISSISSIPPI

In 1860, the majority of Mississippi's population was enslaved, and whites overwhelmingly backed secession. However, in Natchez, the wealthiest city in the state, elites initially opposed secession, fearing that leaving the Union would disrupt their ties to the broader national economy. Natchez reluctantly supported secession in 1861, but the town was forced to surrender to the Union Navy in May 1862. Under Union control, slaveholders were torn. While young men from the city continued to fight for the Confederacy, local planters saw the production of cotton for the Union as an economic necessity. This editorial signaled new willingness to cooperate with the Union.

Any person who is at all acquainted with the state of affairs on the plantations in the neighboring parishes, is aware that large tracts of land which were planted last spring, and have produced good crops of cotton, corn, etc., will be useless to their owners for want of help to harvest their products. The negroes, formerly kept on those plantations have come into the lines, and left the planters to save of their labors as best they may . . . not believing in any occupation from Gen. Banks's forces they made calculations for another full crop, and have got one on their hands. The negroes having asserted their freedom and left their crops, and instead of being a benefit become in part a nuisance, and partially a dead loss for want of help to save it.

Now if these planters could hire negro laborers, as there are comparatively none other to be had, they might save their crops, and carry on their business next year in a more stable and satisfactory manner, as regards being supplied with the necessary help.

We know many who have owned [slaves], will feel strong distaste at being made accessory to the extinction of slavery, hoping that the old order of things may be revived . . . but as there is no probability of such a restoration ever occurring, will it not be wiser and more profitable for them to bury these prejudices and hopes out of sight, and do their best to adapt themselves to the new order of things?

Then the enquiry may be raised, where and how can we hire negroes, and what guaranty can we get that they should stay with us from the planting to the harvesting of a crop is completed? To this we reply, there is quite a large number of negroes within our lines, whom the Provost Marshal would be glad to hire out to persons willing to enter into arrangements with him for that purpose. Of course the negro, in view of the declared policy of the administration, will be considered as *free* by the military authorities, who will maintain a kind of guardianship over these people, and [see that] they are not defrauded of their earnings, cruelly punished, or overtasked.

Natchez Daily Courier, July 3, 1863, reprinted in the *Jackson Mississippian,* October 10, 1863.

41

A POLITICAL PRISONER WRITES TO
ABRAHAM LINCOLN

A southern opponent of the war, William Fitzgerald wrote this letter to Abraham Lincoln while confined in Richmond's Castle Thunder prison. Fitzgerald's letter was mailed by a friend in Virginia and was received at the White House. (Both the Union and Confederacy allowed some mail service through enemy lines during the war.) Lincoln lacked the time to read most of the fifty thousand letters he received during the war, and there is no evidence that he read this one. Fitzgerald died in mid-July 1863. The letter remains in Lincoln's collected papers in the Library of Congress.

Castle Thunder
Richmond, July 4 1863

As a citizen of the United States I take the liberty of addressing you a short letter.

I am now, and for a considerable time have been incarcerated by the Enemies of our Country, in Castle Thunder, Richmond. Here I shall soon die; but before being consigned to my obscure grave, I desire as a Southern man to applaud and commend your efforts in the holy cause in which you are engaged; not only for restoring the Union, but in rending the shackles of Slavery from millions of our fellow beings—Let me assure you that the prayers of thousands in the South ascend to heaven daily for your ultimate success, in the great work—.

The heads of the wicked rebellion, and the public journals of the Country, would have the people of the North and of Europe believe, that the Southern people are unanimously in favor of a new government; but, Sir, a pretension more false was never promulgated—If the sense and will of the people, including the rank and file of the army, could be taken to-day, they would, by an overwhelming majority, declare in favor of the Union—Of the white population of the South more than two thirds of the adult males are nonslave-holders or poor—It is impossible for them to fraternize with such men as Jeff Davis, [William] Lowndes Yancey, [Judah] Benjamin, and their coadjutors—It would be unnatural for them to sympathise with this fratracidal rebellion, or revere an oligarchy founded on slavery, which the rebel leaders are seeking to establish—Slavery has been a curse of the poor white man of the south and he would be mad indeed to desire to perpetuate it—the wealthy planter has ever been the poor mans enemy and oppressor, and the latter would be too generous by half if he disired to increase his foes power over him—You may depend upon it that in general the rich of the South dispise the poor, and the poor in return hate the rich—

True it is that the army of the Confederacy is composed principally of non-Slaveholders but they are not in arms of their own volition

True it is that at the beginning of the war many volunteers from this class were raised; but they did not realize the fact that they were to fight against the United States, against the Union—We are a sensation people; and they were carried away by the excitement of the moment—The leaders induced them to believe that they were merely going to repel another John Brown raid—The deception then successfully practiced by the heartless traitors, enabled them afterward to enforce the conscription, and now the people are powerless—But let the war for the Union be prosecuted, let your armies advance, and wherever they can promis security to the people you will find the masses loyal—

In conclusion I will venture a single suggestion on another point— It would be arrogance and folly in an humble individual like myself to presume to council the chief Magistrate of a great nation but having closely watched the progress of this war, and the policy of your administration, I may be pardoned for expressing the result of my observations, and a single suggestion—

Your Emancipation proclimation opened the grandest issue in this sanguenary struggle, and may prove the heaviest blow dealt the rebellion—But as I understand it, and as it is unwisely interpreted in the South, it frees all Slaves within the territory to which it applies without offering any indemnity to loyal citizens.—In this respect it is wanting—There are many loyal slaveholders in the South, and your proclimation has driven some, and will drive others over to the rebels—I know within my circle of acquaintances several with whome it has had this effect—In my own town two gentlemen, who before the proclimation were regarded as union men, and furnished substitutes to the rebels with great reluctance, immediately after the promulgation of the document, entered the Confederate service, one as a Colonel, and another as captain—Not only were these two men added to the rebel army, but the influence of there example was by no means insignificant—

Since then you cannot desire the innocent to suffer for the misdeeds of the guilty, that the loyal should receive—the wages of treason, let another proclimation be issued, promising loyal citizens of the South reasonable compensation for the slaves liberated, out of the confiscated property of this disloyal, and the two proclimations together will quickly prove, with the assistance of the army now in the field, the heaviest blows, and the death blows of the rebellion—

Such is the belief of your dying, and,
Obediant Servant—

William Fitzgerald to Abraham Lincoln, July 4, 1863, Lincoln Papers, Library of Congress.

42

UNION SOLDIERS LOOT JEFFERSON
DAVIS'S POSSESSIONS

Jefferson Davis owned Brierfield, a plantation in the rich cotton lands of the Mississippi delta. It was vulnerable to Union raiding parties along the Mississippi River, especially after the fall of the Confederate fort at Vicksburg on July 4, 1863. From Richmond, Davis attempted to hide his personal possessions, including his enormous personal library, letters, and fine wines, by transferring them to the residence of Oliver M. Cox, near Jackson, Mississippi. Robert Melvin, a temporary occupant of Cox's house, described a Union raid that followed.

Hinds co. Miss
July 22d. 1863.

DEAR SIR.

As you have without doubt before this had an account through the medium of the Northern Press, of the despoiling of your property, left at the residence of O. B. Cox Esqr of this county; and as your account has doubtless been colored by the exaggerations and embellishments characteristic of Yankee mendacity, I feel it due to myself, as well as to your Excellency, to give you a literal statement of the facts of the case, I having been an eyewitness of the whole transaction from first to last.

On the morning succeeding the intelligence of the surrender of Vicksburg, I was called on by Mr Cox, with the request that I would remove my family, for a temporary sojourn, to his residence, to take, and exercise, a kind of guardianship over the place, and property left on it, as he was going, he knew not where, to be absent he knew not how long. As my wife has been an invalid for many years, the last six confined to her bed; as my residence was about in the center of where we supposed their [the Union] army would march; and Mr Cox's residence was considerably removed, I consented. Mr Cox left on Wednesday I moved in on the same day. He however gave me no intimation that there was any property belonging to your Excellency on the premises nor had I the remotest suspicion of the existence of such property at the time of my removal nor for some time after the Federal troops began to arrive

The secret of its existence however, together with the place of its concealment was betrayed by the treachery of a negro, formerly the property of Mr. Cox, who ran away and went to the Federal army in May last.

The consequence of his treachery was that from the very first of their arrival which was about 10 o'clock on Friday they began to inquire for books, furniture, and wine belonging to your Excellency. (Their exact language was "Old Jeff's" books, furniture and wine) In vain I denied all knowledge of any such property. The assertion was made and repeated again and again that this was your plantation and I your Overseer; my denial being utterly disregarded.

Early in the day on Saturday, Alfred (the negro in question) arrived, when he immediately began to point out place after place where property was concealed. Their first attack was on the books and furniture, boxed up and placed over the dining room. (I presume [you] know where and how the property was secured) Soon as the discovery was made of anything bearing your Excellency's name the news ran like fire in the prairie and the crowd of thousands was soon swelled to tens of thousands. Boxes were torn open and emptied of their contents; books and papers were strewed over the yard and scattered through the woods for miles; fine carpets were cut to pieces and carried off for saddle blankets and saddle covers fine window curtains were taken for tent blankets; and in fact everything useful or ornamental was plundered and destroyed with a ruthlessness worthy of Attila himself.

During all this scene of desolation I was not suffered even to look at the theatre of their havoc being myself under guard, having the bayonets of three soldiers pointed at my breast all the time; and being threatened with the most shocking imprecations not to move on pain of instant death.

Of all things taken by them they appeared to exalt more in some walking sticks than anything else except the wine.

The distruction commenced on Saturday and continued without any interruption except for a few hours in the latter part of the night until about noon on Monday when one of their Generals came with a wagon and team (six mules) and carried off everything he thought worth removing. I was then permitted to look over the general wreck for the first time. I found a small walnut card table, one leaf split off, a small writing case (Rosewood I think) top and bottom torn off doors torn to pieces and otherwise much injured and defaced, two sofas one hair cloth seat the other velvet. The only injury I have as yet perceived done to them is the seat of the hair cloth sofa has been somewhat cut up either to gratify a petty malice or in the hope of finding something concealed, the velvet one is untouched.

There were some fine chairs in the parlor and elsewhere on which my daughter found the name "President Davis" in large letters on cotton cloth She slipped noiselessly through the crowd, succeeded in tearing off and destroying the name and then claimed them as her own. She thus saved them. A marble statue I claimed as the likeness of my dead child by which means I saved it. Otherwise it would have been broken to pieces and the fragments sent North as trophies. I have just finished boxing up the books and papers and truly I find it a much easier matter for a thousand men to tear up and destroy than for one to follow after and restore order out of their confusion

In the load carried off by Genl. [Hugh] Ewing there was a considerable amount of the personal property both of Mr Cox and my own but it was useless to remonstrate.

During the first two days (Saturday and Sunday) the negro Alfred looked on the general destruction with perfect fiendish delight

Among the evidences of petty malice a book was found containing Your Excellency's likeness; this the soldiers stabbed as often as they could find a piece of the paper large enough to receive the point of a knife

In conclusion I crave pardon of your Excellency for the prolix epistle I have inflicted on you; also for the paper I have used. It was all I could procure. And now I conclude [by describing] myself Your excellency's Most Obt. Sevt.

ROBT. MELVIN

P.S. As all mail facilities have been destroyed I shall have to wait an opportunity of sending this by hand. R. M.

The Papers of Jefferson Davis, vol. 9, *January–September 1863,* ed. Lynda Lasswell Crist and Mary Seaton Dix (Baton Rouge: Louisiana State Univ. Press, 1997), 299–301.

43

A FORMER SOLDIER BEGINS TO FARM
(THREE DOCUMENTS)

A North Carolina lawyer and plantation owner, Walter Lenoir joined the Confederate Army roughly a year after the war began. After losing a leg on the battlefield, he returned home to a small mountain farm in western North Carolina. In this letter, he commented on slavery's role in the conflict.

Crab Orchard, July 23d, 1863

Dear Brother,

The course of events and my reflections of late have led me to modify my opinions as to some of the darker and more horrid aspects of the war, growing out of the subject of slavery. You know that I have never regarded Lincoln's Proclamation as making of itself much substantial difference in the conduct of the war. The Yankees have gone on since doing just what they were doing before, and in the same manner, so far as the slaves and slavery is concerned.

You know too that I have not dreaded their attempts to arm the slaves, believing that their presence in their armies would be a cause of weakness instead of strength, and that they would be shrewd enough to know that or soon find it out, and limit the experiment to such bounds as they thought would be sufficient to keep the South in a state of alarm. I did think, however, that to the extent that they were introduced, it would make the war more horrid, because I supposed that our men would refuse to capture them when found fighting, as well as the white officers who commanded them. In this I find I was mistaken. Our troops capture negro soldiers and their officers and treat them as they do the others. And this I have no doubt now will continue to be the case to the end of the war. I still think, for the reasons that I have already mentioned, that there will be but little use made by the Yankees of their negro soldiers, though I see that Gen. Banks tries to make them out quite valiant. It is so natural to man to fight that it is possible that even the negro diciplined and led by white men may stand fire better than we of the South have supposed. But even if this is so, amalgamation in the ranks with them as well as every where else is so very unnatural that even Yankee fanaticism will fail in the attempt. That, however, is not the point which I set out to state, which was merely that the addition of negro troops to the Yankee army would not as I now think prevent them from being taken prisoners by our troops when in their power, as their mean white associates now are.

My views have undergone a still greater change on another and much more important point in this connexion. I have as you know never thought that the Yankees would succeed in liberating our slaves. I believe that God over rules the affairs of nations, and that He will not suffer the Yankees to perpetrate so great a crime as that against us and their species. But while we know that God is just and merciful and does all things right, we know that His ways are not our ways, and are past finding out, and often seem very mysterious to our imperfect perceptions. We are not certain therefore beyond a doubt but that it may be his righteous will that our enemies may succeed in this. Looking at the possibility of such a thing, and considering it in the light of human reason and experience, I took it almost for granted at first that such a forcible emancipation would lead to scenes of horrid massacre and butchery; that the negroes finding freedom in their grasp, and having their passions inflamed by the fierce teachings of abolitionists would attempt to slay their masters, and that they in turn would be compelled to destroy the negroes. . . . But I now believe that if the Yankees succeed in subjugating the white people of the South and freeing the negroes it will be without any massacres except such as are now taking place upon the battle field. There will be no rising upon the non-combatant men, women or children. Those of us who choose to see it will see their Yankee masters set the negroes free and then govern them and their fellow citizens, their late masters and mistresses, as well as the people of subjugated are governed by other enlightened nations. Bad as the Yankees are they would not wish the whites of the South to be massacred by the negroes and would not permit it. . . . If the Yankees are strong enough to put down our fierce and strong fight for independence they will be strong enough to govern the negroes afterwards, and I have little doubt for my part that if the South is subdued by the North it will be as well governed and prosperous as Jamaica. Not a very tempting prospect truly, not one that I would expect to remain to witness if I could pay or beg my way to some other country. . . .

The peace party which seems to be growing rapidly now at the North will then become stronger and more clamerous and I hope that the North will begin to conclude that the war is "played out." You know I thought last winter we would have more and harder fighting this year than any before, and that there would not be much afterwards. I still think so.

Your brother
Walter [Lenoir]

As the war dragged on, draft resisters and deserters openly defied a government that became increasingly weak in western North Carolina. However, many remained loyal, including Lenoir and his family.

July 25, 1863

Dear Uncle

Well Uncle Walt I must tell you how domestic we have grown since the war broke out. We have learned to spin weave &c &c. Mary and Mother spun filling enough for a fine piece of cloth and it is mighty nice and soft. Mary is a first rate spinner; she can beat me all to pieces. We have kept two looms going constantly all summer and spring, nearly. I guess the weaving operations will be suspended for a time now. I have to go to school, and Millie will have to sew so there will be no one to weave but Betsy. I am sorry to tell you of the Union sentiment existing in this county, among the women as well as the men; the women write to their husbands to leave the army and come home and that's the reason that so many of them are deserting. They have a regular union company up at trap hill! March under an old dirty United States rag! &c. Some of the people about here actually rejoiced at the death of Genl Jackson! Oh! It makes me so mad to think about that I just want to fight. I wish the Yankees had the last one of them.

Your Affectionate Niece
Julia P Gwynne

Lenoir's neighbor, Joseph Norwood, bemoaned the desperate state of pro-Confederate forces in the mountains of North Carolina.

August 13, 1863

My Dear Walter
They have a terrible state of things upon the Tennessee particularly in Watauga [County]. There is a band of robbers & villains who are constantly plundering the people in the night, when resolute and prepared they succeed in driving them off, but a man is occasionally killed on either side. Some ten days ago they attacked the house of Paul Farthing—his brother Young being there[.] They resisted and fired upon them out of the house & a skirmish ensued[.] Thomas Farthing heard the firing from his house and hurried over with his gun but unfortunately was discovered & fired upon by a guard stationed on the road side—two balls passing through his heart. You may imagine my distress knowing the high estimation in which I held him. I regarded him decidedly the first man in the County—& I think he was a fast friend of our family. The band was headed by a man by the name of Guy[.] he has been arrested & released here-

tofore—They go in bands of 12 to 14—Nine of Paul Farthing's family were hurt & they found a good deal of blood about the porch & corner of the house; but as they always carry off their wounded the damage done the robbers was not ascertained—the same party robbed Mr. Evans' house while he was down here, carrying off about four five hundred dollars worth of his & Mr. Skiles's effects—They put his wife under guard & rummaged the house thoroughly—expecting to find money. Evans has since moved his family down here & occupies the Methodist Parsonage.

I have terrible forebodings at times—not that I think that we are not able to defend ourselves and achieve our independence—but fear that the whole strength of the country can not be got out. The men who have heretofore avoided the fight & by coming forward at this crisis & encouraging the remaining conscripts and deserters might restore confidence are increasing the difficulty by crying out for peace which means submission—In the meantime desertion is rife[.] the men regard their money as worthless & the government is unable to remedy its evil. Thomas says he is seen them give $10 for a water mellon.

Your affectionate
Jos C. Norwood

Lenoir Papers, Wilson Library, University of North Carolina.

—— 44 ——

A PRISONER OF WAR ENCOUNTERS
SOUTHERN WOMEN

Union soldier William H. Tillson, of Company E, 84th Illinois Regiment, was captured in 1863. Confederate authorities took him to Libby Prison in Richmond by a circuitous route, probably due to the poor state of Confederate railroads. His wartime account includes this description of interactions between Union prisoners and southern women. In poor health, he was exchanged for a southern prisoner in April of 1864. He was discharged from the Union Army due to his wounds on September 22, 1864.

Augusta 6th Day Sept 26th 1863

This morning gives us a good view all around. The yard is a beautiful shady place. The town is beautiful well laid off shady level and has waterworks. We passed through it as we were leaving it. And having crossed the Savannah River find our selves in the rebellious state of South Carolina[.] The hot bed of treason. The corn crops were poor[.] saw much yellow pine timber and a good deal of swampy land[.] The water along at places was a black color[.] Before reaching Branchville, an incident occured. At one place along the road there was quite a number of Aristocratic young and elderly ladies came to gaze at us[.] Some of the boys stopped to get some water. The young ladies at first were shy or pretended to be afraid. But it was not long before they were not so[.] One of them in particular was talking quite lively and familliarly with one or two of our young men. By appearances they were having a pretty lively chat. So familliar that one of the ladies got hold of a novel and would not give it back. Just then the whistle blew. He snatched for the book[.] But she clung to it and insisted upon keeping it[.] And she did keep it, Saying she wished to keep it to remember him and the yankees. The little quarrell caused quite a shout and laugh[.] The boys shouted here is your pet yan-kee—Your yankee prisoner & c and then off for South Carolina! The grade being high our poor iron horse was retarded. The night was very cold.

William H. Tillson diary, Southern Historical Collection, Wilson Library, University of North Carolina.

THE CONFEDERATE WAR DEPARTMENT AND
THE IMPRESSMENT OF SLAVES

The Confederate military used slave labor to build fortifications, drive wagons, and cook meals. Ironically, in a war to preserve human bondage, some slave owners viewed even temporary wartime use of their human property—known as impressment—as a patently unfair form of taxation.

CONFEDERATE STATES OF AMERICA, WAR DEPARTMENT
Richmond, November 26, 1863.
His Excellency, JEFFERSON DAVIS,
    President Confederate States of America

SIR:
    I have the honor to submit the following report:——
. . . To some extent, likewise, the necessity of details might be obviated by some organized system of impressing or engaging the labor of free negroes and slaves where they could be made available. The effort to do this, by the temptation of interests of owners, has been generally found to be unavailing. In many of the Government works, where the unskilled labor of slaves would be most available, exposure to the seductions or attacks of the enemy are dreaded by owners, who are averse to having them removed from their personal supervision and influence. To command slaves, therefore, in anything like the number required for the many works of Government to which they could be applied, compulsion in some form would be necessary. The use of negroes may, likewise, swell the number of men in arms in the field by substituting teamsters, cooks, and other camp employees who are

now largely supplied from the ranks. This policy has heretofore met the approbation of Congress, and been embodied in the act approved April 21, 1862. No provision, however, was made to procure the negroes for these offices, and from the causes mentioned, although their utility has been recognized, they could not be obtained by voluntary engagements of service or hire from their owners.

There may be difficulties and embarrassments in enforcing the service of slaves, but they might be overcome on the principle of impressing them as property, or of requiring contributions from their owners of certain quotas for public service, as has been done for works of public defense. The wickedness and malignity of our enemies have certainly placed [a] considerable number of negroes, almost of necessity, at the control of our Government. To favor the pusillanimity of their people, as well the better to advance the nefarious ends of their unjust warfare, they have adopted as their deliberate policy the employment of the slaves as soldiers in their Army. They have already formed numerous regiments of the slaves they have seduced or forced from their masters, and the statement has been boastfully made in their public prints that they [the Union] already have some 30,000 negro troops in arms. It is now an ascertained fact that as they overrun any portion of our territory they draw off, often by compulsion, the most efficient male slaves and place them in their negro regiments; and when they have established anywhere a temporary occupation, they practice a regular system of compulsory recruiting from the slaves within their reach. Not merely, therefore, for the purpose of preserving to the Confederacy this valuable labor, thus abstracted, but from the plainer necessity of preventing the enemy from recruiting their armies with our slaves, it becomes a clear obligation on the military authorities of the Confederacy to remove from any district exposed to be occupied or overrun by the enemy the effective male slaves.

Were there any white population within our country so affected by the enemy as to afford recruits to their Army, there could be neither doubt nor delay in removing them to a secure distance on the approach of hostile forces, and surely the obligation is even more clear in regard to the slaves, whose employment by the enemy as soldiers converts them from valuable laborers into savage instruments of an atrocious war against our people and their institutions. All male slaves capable of arms, in such cases should, on the approach of the enemy, be at once removed by military authority to more secure districts, where they may be reclaimed by their masters, or, on their failure to do so, be employed on reasonable terms of hire by the Government. In this way, it is probable, a large number of efficient negroes may be obtained to supply the details from the Army for all unskilled labor, and also to liberate for arms the soldiers now engaged in unwarlike duties to the trains and camps of our armies. While it may be difficult to obtain the precise numbers that may, from these various sources, be thrown into our armies, there can be no doubt they would be swelled considerably beyond their present numbers, and constitute an army larger, as well as more effective, than any we have yet mustered. In view of the increasing repugnance of the enemy to furnish recruits to their Army, and the falling hopes it indicates, it is almost certain that manifestation of strength and resolution on the part of the people of the Confederacy would soon be decisive of the struggle. When all the disastrous consequences of long, wasting warfare are weighed and the mighty issues, to ourselves and our posterity, dependent on our success are realized, and it is apparent our people have only with united wills and a supreme effort to put forth their entire strength to assure the prize of peace and independence, should there be misgiving or hesitancy even in adopting all the means requisite to summon forth the full number of our population of age and ability for arms, and to hurl them against the invading foe? The only inquiry, it is hoped, will be for the agencies that can most speedily accomplish the desired marshaling.

James Seddon to Jefferson Davis, November 26, 1863, *The War of the Rebellion: A Compilation of the Official Records of the Union and Confederate Armies* (Washington, D.C.: Government Printing Office, 1880–1901), series 4, vol. 2, 998–99.

46

WILLIAM T. SHERMAN AND HARD WAR

Just before the Civil War began, William Tecumseh Sherman, a West Point graduate, worked at a Louisiana military school. Sherman had no sympathy for abolitionists, but despised secessionists even more. After Louisiana left the Union, he returned to the army. By 1863, Sherman became the most visible proponent of "hard war" tactics in the Union military. He advocated war against not only the Confederate Army, but also its civilian supporters.

HEADQUARTERS DEPARTMENT OF THE TENNESSEE,
Nashville, December 21, 1863.
Maj. Gen. JOHN A. LOGAN,
Commanding Fifteenth Army Corps, Bridgeport:

Dear General:

I got here last night, stay over to-day, and go to Louisville to-morrow. I have seen General [Ulysses] Grant, and General [Grenville] Dodge is also here. I think I can see the drift of events for a short time ahead, and you should know them. I will go home for Christmas (the first for more than twenty years), but on the 2d of January will start for Cairo, and in concert with Admiral [David Dixon] Porter must do something to check the boldness of our enemy in attacking boats on the Mississippi.

To secure the safety of the navigation of the Mississippi River I would slay millions. On that point I am not only insane, but mad. Fortunately, the great West is with me there. I think I see one or two quick blows that will astonish the natives of the South, and will convince them that, though to stand behind a big cotton-wood and shoot at a passing boat is good sport and safe, it may still reach and kill their friends and families hundreds of miles off. For every bullet shot at a steam-boat, I would shoot a thousand 30-pounder Parrotts into even helpless towns on Red, Ouachita, Yazoo, or wherever a boat can float or soldier march. Well, I think in all January and part of February I can do something in this line.

Your friend,
W. T. SHERMAN
Major-General

The War of the Rebellion: A Compilation of the Official Records of the Union and Confederate Armies (Washington, D.C.: Government Printing Office, 1880–1901), series 1, vol. 31, part 3, 459–60.

47

A REFUGEE BEMOANS THE BRUTALITY OF THE WAR

A native of Maryland, nineteen-year-old Priscilla Bond married a wealthy Louisiana planter just before the Civil War began. Her husband quickly volunteered to fight for the Confederacy. As Union forces advanced into Louisiana, she was forced to leave her home and settle with relatives.

Tuesday, [December] 29th [1863]

. . . I went around to Mrs. Patrick's. Old irish John was there drunk—If there is anything, or anybody I am afraid of it is a drunken man. I got away as soon as I could. The Confederates carried a young man from the town over the bayou—I suppose will take him to Lafayette. They shot him several weeks since through the face, inflicting a dreadful wound—but not fatal. He deserted our army last fall or spring & went to the Yankees, & several weeks since they caught him as a spy—he would not halt—is the reason they shot him. I suppose he will be dealt with according to Law. If the Yankees come now I guess they will nearly take up the town. If the soldiers are about New Year's, Mrs. Maxwell intends giving them a dinner & a ball at night. The old year is fast coming to a close—Oh! how many sad bleeding hearts this year has made! May God in his infinite mercy put a stop shortly to this miserable war! It does not appear to me like any other period of life I ever spent. The time speeds by rapidly—the same old routine is gone through every day. Sometimes life is very monotonous—then again, startling change takes place so rapidly that it fills one with intense excitement & expectation as to what shall next appear.

Kimberly Harrison, ed., *A Maryland Bride in the Deep South: The Civil War Diary of Priscilla Bond* (Baton Rouge: Louisiana State Univ. Press, 2006), 250.

1864

48

A SOUTHERN WOMAN'S DESPAIR

Judith McGuire was married to John P. McGuire, founder of a semi-nary in Alexandria, Virginia. She wrote an eloquent diary of her experience of being forced from her home. During the war she worked as a clerk in the Commissary Department in Richmond. In this passage from her diary McGuire discussed her grief over the death of a cousin.

January 1, 1864.

A melancholy pause in my diary. After returning from church on the night of the 18th, a telegram was handed me from Prof. [John] Minor, of the University of Virginia, saying, "Come at once, Colonel [Raleigh] Colston is extremely ill." After the first shock was over, I wrote an explanatory note to Major [Richard Henry] Brewer, why I could not be at the office the next day, packed my trunk, and was in the cars by seven in the morning. . . . After ten days of watching and nursing, amid alternate hopes and fears, we saw our friend Dr. [Socrates] Maupin close our darling's eyes, on the morning of the 23rd; and on Christmas-day, a military escort laid him among many brother soldiers in the Cemetery of the University of Virginia. He died in the faith of Christ, and with the glorious hope of immortality. His poor mother is heart-stricken, but she, together with his sisters, and one dearer still, had the blessed, and what is now the rare privilege, of soothing and nursing him in his last hours. To them, and to us all, his life seemed as a part of our own. His superior judgment and affectionate temper made him the guide of the whole family. To them his loss can never be supplied. . . .

Thus we bury, one by one, the dearest, the brightest, the best of our domestic circles. Now, in our excitement, while we are scattered, and many of us homeless, the separations are poignant, nay, overwhelming; but how can we estimate the sadness of heart which will pervade the South when the war is over, and we are again gathered together around our family hearths and altars, and find the circles broken? One and another gone. Sometimes the father and husband, the beloved head of the household, in whom was centered all that made life dear. Again the eldest son and brother of the widowed home, to whom all looked for guidance and direction; or, perhaps, that bright youth, on whom we had not ceased to look at still as a child, whose fair, beardless cheek we had but now been in the habit of smoothing with our hands in fondness—one to whom mother and sisters would always give the good-night kiss, as his peculiar due, and repress the sigh that would arise at the thought that college or business days had almost come to take him from us. And then we will remember the mixed feeling of hope and pride when we first saw this household pet don his jacket of gray and shoulder his musket for the field; how we would be bright and cheerful before him, and turn to our chambers to weep oceans of tears when he is fairly gone. And does he, too, sleep his last sleep? Does our precious one fill a hero's grave? O God! help us, for the wail is in the whole land!

Judith W. McGuire, *Diary of a Southern Refugee during the War, by a Lady of Virginia* (New York: E. J. Hale and Son, 1868), 249–50.

49

CONFEDERATE EMANCIPATION:
A PROPOSAL

*General Patrick Cleburne, an Irish immigrant, moved to Arkansas
in 1849, where he became a successful lawyer. Fighting in the Army
of Tennessee, he recognized that the Confederacy lacked a sufficient
white population base to prevail in a lengthy conflict. Therefore, he
proposed a radical step: the recruitment of black soldiers to fight for
the rebellion. Jefferson Davis immediately rejected the secret proposal.*

[JANUARY 3, 1864]
COMMANDING GENERAL, THE CORPS, DIVISION, BRIGADE, AND
REGIMENTAL COMMANDERS OF THE ARMY OF TENNESSEE.

Apart from the assistance that home and foreign prejudice against
slavery has given to the North, slavery is a source of great strength to
the enemy in a purely military point of view, by supplying him with
an army from our granaries; but it is our most vulnerable point, a
continued embarrassment, and in some respects an insidious weakness. Wherever slavery is once seriously disturbed, whether by the
actual presence or the approach of the enemy, or even by a cavalry
raid, the whites can no longer with safety to their property openly
sympathize with our cause. The fear of their slaves is continually
haunting them, and from silence and apprehension many of these
soon learn to wish the war stopped on any terms. The next stage is
to take the oath to save property, and they become dead to us, if not
open enemies. To prevent raids we are forced to scatter our forces,
and are not free to move and strike like the enemy; his vulnerable

points are carefully selected and fortified depots. Ours are found in every point where there is a slave to set free. . . .

The measure will at one blow strip the enemy of foreign sympathy and assistance, and transfer them to the South; it will dry up two of his three sources of recruiting; it will take from his negro army the only motive it could have to fight against the South, and will probably cause much of it to desert over to us; it will deprive his cause of the powerful stimulus of fanaticism, and will enable him to see the rock on which his so-called friends are piloting him. The immediate effect of the emancipation and enrollment of negroes on the military strength of the South would be: To enable us to have armies numerically superior to those of the North, and a reserve of any size we might think necessary; to enable us to take the offensive, move forward, and forage on the enemy. It would open to us in prospective another and almost untouched source of supply, and furnish us with the means of preventing temporary disaster, and carrying on a protracted struggle. It would instantly remove all the vulnerability, embarrassment, and inherent weakness which result from slavery. The approach of the enemy would no longer find every household surrounded by spies; the fear that sealed the master's lips and the avarice that has, in so many cases, tempted him practically to desert us would alike be removed. There would be no recruits awaiting the enemy with open arms, no complete history of every neighborhood with ready guides, no fear of insurrection in the rear, or anxieties for the fate of loved ones when our armies moved forward. The chronic irritation of hope deferred would be joyfully ended with the negro, and the sympathies of his whole race would be due to his native South. It would restore confidence in an early termination of the war with all its inspiring consequences, and even if contrary to all expectations the enemy should succeed in over-running the South, instead of finding a cheap, ready-made means of holding it down, he would find a common hatred and thirst for vengeance, which would break into acts at every favorable opportunity, would prevent him from settling on our lands, and render the South a very unprofitable conquest. It would remove forever all selfish taint from our cause and place independence above every question of property. The very magnitude of the sacrifice itself, such as no nation has ever voluntarily made before, would appal[l] our enemies, destroy his spirit and his finances, and fill our hearts with a pride and singleness of purpose which would clothe us with new strength in battle. Apart from all other aspects of the question, the necessity for more fighting men is upon us. We can only get a sufficiency by making the negro share the danger and hardships of war. If we arm and train him and make him fight for the country in her hour of dire distress, every consideration of principle and policy demand that we should set him and his whole race who side with us free. It is a first principle with mankind that he who offers his life in defense of the State should receive from her in return his freedom and his happiness, and we believe in acknowledgement of this principle. The Constitution of the Southern States has reserved to their respective governments the power to free slaves for meritorious services to the State. It is politic besides. For many years, ever since the agitation of the subject of slavery commenced, the negro has been dreaming of freedom, and his vivid imagination has surrounded that condition with so many gratifications that it has become the paradise of his hopes. To attain it he will tempt dangers and difficulties not exceeded by the bravest soldier in the field. The hope of freedom is perhaps the only moral incentive that can be applied to him in his present condition. It would be preposterous then to expect him to fight against it with any degree of enthusiasm, therefore we must bind him to our cause by no doubtful bonds; we must leave no possible loop-hole for treachery to creep in.

P. R. Cleburne, major-general, commanding division; D. C. Govan, brigadier-general; John R. Murray, colonel Fifth Arkansas; G. F. Baucom, colonel Eighth Arkansas; Peter Snyder, lieutenant-colonel, commanding Sixth and Seventh Arkansas; E. Warfield, lieutenant-colonel, Second Arkansas; M. P. Lowrey, brigadier-general; A. B. Hardcastle, colonel Thirty-second and Forty-Fifth Mississippi; F. A. Ashford, major, Sixteenth Alabama; Rich. J. Person, major, Third and Fifth Confederate; G. S. Deakins, major, Thirty-fifth and Eighth

Tennesseee; J. H. Colquitt, captain, commanding Seventh Texas; J. H. Kelly, brigadier-general, commanding Cavalry Division.

The War of the Rebellion: A Compilation of the Official Records of the Union and Confederate Armies (Washington, D.C.: Government Printing Office, 1880–1901), series 1, vol. 52, part 2, 586–92.

50

"THIS IS OUR COUNTRY": A MEETING OF FORMER SLAVES

In 1862, forces under Ulysses S. Grant seized control of the Tennessee and Cumberland Rivers, making Confederate rule of Memphis untenable. By the end of the war, twenty thousand escaped slaves from Tennessee had served in the U. S. Army. The following resolutions were passed by a massive assembly of Memphis freedmen in January 1864.

Resolved, That we hail with feelings of joy and gratitude to Almighty God, that we have the exalted privilege of meeting together, for the purpose of offering tribute and honor to one of the most magnanimous and brilliant chapters written in the nineteenth century.

Resolved, That we greet the dawn of this beautiful and ever memorable day; and we trust that our children will cherish it until truth, and honor shall cease to be revered among the civilized nations of the earth.

Resolved, That the respect to his excellency, the President of the United States, and the admiration we cherish for the gallant army and navy that have born their glittering arms, backed by their courageous hearts, in triumph over hundreds of battle-fields, call upon us to-day to pledge ourselves as colored men to fill the ranks made vacant by our colored brothers, who have fallen so bravely upon the various fields of strife.

Resolved, That we recommend every colored man, capable of performing military duty, both North and South, to enlist forthwith in the army and navy of the United States, where he can successfully perform his duty to his God, his country, and his fellow men.

Resolved, As this is our country, and we are citizens of the United States, in the eloquent language of Attorney-General [Edward Bates]; therefore we are willing to defend them with life and limb; and after protecting them with our guns, we humbly pray God that there may be generosity enough left to protect us in our native land.

Resolved, That we recommend the colored people everywhere in the United States to stand by the Government, to be true to the stars and stripes.

Resolved, That we recommend the benevolent associations of the North to send us teachers, who are known to be our true and devoted friends.

The Liberator, January 29, 1864.

51

"YOU GOT MY HOG!": A THEFT BY CONFEDERATE SOLDIERS

In 1861, Tennessee's Private Sam Watkins joined a company of 120 men. By the end of the war the company had been reduced to seven. His eloquent memoir, first published in 1882, is one of the few by a rank-and-file Confederate soldier. Watkins's book combined an unflinching realism and a keen sense of irony in describing the horrors of war. In this passage, he described an encounter between soldiers and an impoverished southern woman near Dalton, Georgia, in the winter of 1863–1864.

One day, a party of "us privates" concluded we would go across the Conasauga river on a raid. We crossed over in a canoe. After traveling for some time, we saw a neat looking farmhouse, and sent one of the party forward to reconnoiter. He returned in a few minutes and announced that he had found a fine fat sow in a pen near the house. Now, the plan we formed was for two of us to go into the house and keep the inmates interested and the other was to toll and drive off the hog. I was one of the party which went into the house. There was no one there but an old lady and her sick and widowed daughter. They invited us in very pleasantly and kindly, and soon prepared us a very nice and good dinner. The old lady told us of all her troubles and trials. Her husband had died before the war, and she had three sons in the army, two of whom had been killed, and the youngest, who had been conscripted, was taken with the camp fever and died in the hospital at Atlanta, and she had nothing to subsist upon, after eating up what they then had. I was much interested, and remained a little while after my comrade had left. I soon went out, having made up my mind to have nothing to do with the whole affair. I did not know how to act. I was in a bad fix. I had heard the gun fire and knew its portent. I knew the hog was dead, and when I left the road, and soon overtook my two comrades with the hog, which had been skinned and cut up, and was being carried on a pole between them. I did not know what to do. In looking back I saw the old lady coming in screaming at the top of her voice, "You got my hog!" It was too late to back out now. We had the hog, and had to make the most of it, even if we did ruin a needy and destitute family. We went on until we came to the Conasauga river, when lo and behold! the canoe was on the other side of the river. It was dark then, and getting darker, and what was to be done we did not know. The weather was as cold as blue blazes, and spitting snow from the northwest. That river had to be crossed that night. I undressed and determined to swim it, and went in, but the little thin ice at the bank cut my feet. I waded in a little further, but soon found I would cramp if I tried to swim it. I came out and put my clothes on, and thought of the gate about a mile back. We went back and took the gate off its hinges and carried it to the river and put it in the water, but soon found out that all three of us could not ride on it; so one of the party got on it and started across. He did very well until he came to the other bank, which was a high bluff, and if he got off the center of the gate it would capsize and he would get a ducking. He could not get off the gate. I told him to pole the gate to the bank, so that one side would rest on the bank, and then make a quick run for the bank. He thought he had got the gate about the right place and then made a run, and the gate went under and so did he, in water ten feet deep. My comrade, Fount C., who was with me on the bank, laughed, I thought, until he had hurt himself; but with me, I assure you, it was a mighty sickly grin, and with the other one, Barkley J., it was anything but a laughing matter. To me he seemed a hero. Barkley did [set] about to liberate me from a very unpleasant position. He soon returned with the canoe, and we crossed the river with the hog. We worried and tugged with it, and got it to camp just before daylight.

I had a guilty conscience, I assure you. The hog was cooked, but I did not eat a piece of it. I felt that I had rather starve, and I believe that it would have choked me to death if I had attempted it.

A short time after work an old citizen from Maury county visited me. My father sent me, by him, a silver watch—which I am wearing today—and eight hundred dollars in old issue Confederate money. I took two hundred dollars of the money, and had it funded for new issue, 33 1/3 cents discount. The other six hundred I sent to Vance Thompson, then on duty at Montgomery, with instructions to send it to my brother, Dave Watkins, Uncle Asa Freeman, and J. E. Dixon, all of whom were in Wheeler's cavalry, at some other point—I knew not where. After getting my money, I found that I had 133.33 1/3. I could not rest. I took one hundred dollars, new issue, and going by my lone self back to the old lady's house, I said, "Madam, some soldiers were here a short time ago, and took your hog. I was one of that party, and I wish to pay you for it. What was it worth? "Well, sir," says she, "money is of no value to me; I cannot get any article that I wish; I would much rather have the hog." Says I, "Madam, that is an impossibility; your hog is dead and eat up, and I have come to pay you for it." The old lady's eyes filled with tears. She said that she was perfectly willing to give the soldiers everything she had, and if she thought it had done us any good, she would not charge anything for it.

"Well," says I, "Madam, here is a hundred dollars, new issue, Confederate bill. Will this pay you for your hog?" "Well, sir," she says, drawing herself up to full height, her cheeks flushed and her eyes flashing, "I do not want your money. I would feel that it was blood money." I saw that there was no further use to offer it to her. I sat down by the fire and the conversation turned upon other subjects.

I helped the old lady catch a chicken (an old hen—about the last she had) for dinner, went with her in the garden and pulled a bunch of escalots, brought two buckets of water, and cut and lodged enough wood to last several days.

After a while, she invited me to dinner, and after dinner I sat down by her side, took her old hand in mine, and told her the whole affair of the hog, from beginning to end; how sorry I was, and how I did not eat any of that hog; that I felt bad about it, and if she would take it, it would ease my conscience. I laid the money on the table and left. I have never in my life made a raid upon anybody else.

Samuel R. Watkins, *"Co. Aytch": Maury Grays, First Tennessee Regiment, Or, A Side Show of the Big Show* (New York: Times Printing Company, 1900), 113–17.

52

JEFFERSON DAVIS'S FUGITIVE SLAVE

When the war began, a third of the residents of Richmond, the Confederate capital, were enslaved. After Union victories at Gettysburg and Vicksburg in the summer of 1863, dwindling Confederate forces found themselves on the defensive. Richmond suffered from a lack of basic supplies and a growing refugee problem. In this context, slaves became increasingly restive, and even Jefferson Davis's household felt the consequences.

February 15th [1864]

The President is unfortunate in his servants, as the following from the *Dispatch* would seem:

"Another of President Davis's Negroes Runs Away"

On Saturday night last the police were informed of the fact that Cornelius, a Negro man in the employ of President Davis, had run away. Having received some clew of his whereabouts, they succeeded in finding him in a few hours after receiving the information of his escape, and lodged him in the upper station house. When caught, there was found on his person snacks enough, consisting of cold chicken, ham, preserves, bread, etc., to last him for a long journey, and a large sum of money he had stolen from his master. Some time after being locked up, he called the keeper of the prison to give him some water, and as that gentleman incautiously opened the door of his cell to wait on him, Cornelius knocked him down and made his escape. Mr. Peter Everett, the only watchman present, [set] off after him; but before running many steps stumbled and fell, injuring himself severely."

John B. Jones, *A Rebel War Clerk's Diary,* vol. 2 (Philadelphia: Lippincott and Co., 1866), 150.

53

A FORMER SLAVE DESCRIBES A DEATH IN
HIS MASTER'S FAMILY

When he was a young man, Louis Hughes was purchased by a Mississippi slaveholder, Edward McGee, whom he called "Boss." Hughes worked for McGee as a domestic servant who also ran errands. The McGee family included "Mack," a young soldier. Dr. Henry Dandridge, who figures in this passage, was related to the McGees by marriage. It was unusual for a slave to feel genuine affection for one of his master's family. Hughes's book has the ring of veracity. Yet, as in all memoirs, the views expressed here may have been shaped by the passage of time.

In the afternoon, when all were seated in the library reading, and I was in the dining room, finishing up my work, I happened to look out of the window, and saw the messenger coming up the graveled walk. I went out to meet him. "Telegram for Mrs. McGee," he said. I took it to her; and, reading it without a word, she passed it to the next member of the family, and so it was passed around until all had read it except Mrs. Dandridge. When it was handed to her, I saw, at a glance, that it contained for her the most sorrowful tidings. As she read she became livid, and when she finished she covered her face with her handkerchief, giving a great, heavy sob. By this time the whole family was crying and screaming: "Oh! our Mack is killed." "Mars, Mack is killed," was echoed by the servants, in tones of heart-felt sorrow, for he was an exceptional young man. Every one loved him—both whites and blacks. The affection of the slaves for him bordered on reverence, and this was true not alone of his father's slaves, but all of those who knew him. This telegram was from Boss, and announced that he would be home the next day with the remains. Mrs. Farrington at once wrote to old Master Jack and to Dr. Dandridge, telling them of Mack's death and to come at once. After I mailed those letters nothing unusual happened during the afternoon, and the house was wrapped in silence and gloom. On the following morning I went for the mail as usual, but there was nothing new. At noon, the remains of the much beloved young man arrived at our station, accompanied by Boss and Dr. Henry Dandridge, brother of the father of the deceased, who was a surgeon in the rebel army. I went to the station with another servant, to assist in bringing the body to the house. We carried it into the back parlor, and, after all had been made ready, we proceeded to wash and dress it. He had lain on the battlefield two days before he was found, and his face was as black as a piece of coal; but Dr. Henry Dandridge, with his ready tact, suggested the idea of painting it. I was there to assist in whatever way they needed me. After the body was all dressed, and the face painted, cheeks tinted with a rosy hue, to appear as he always did in life, the look was natural and handsome. We were all the afternoon employed in this sad work, and it was not until late in the evening that his father and mother came down to view the body for the first time. I remember, as they came down the broad stairs together, the sorrow-stricken yet calm look of those people. Mrs. Dandridge was very calm—her grief was too great for her to scream as the others did when they went in. She stood and looked at her Mack; then turning to Boss, she said: "Cousin Eddie, how brave he was! He died for his country." Poor, sorrowing, misguided woman! It was not for his country he died, but for the perpetuation of the cruel, the infamous system of human slavery. All the servants were allowed to come in and view the body. Many sad tears were shed by them. Some of the older slaves clasped their hands, as if in mute prayer, and exclaimed, as they passed by the coffin: "He was a loving boy." It seems that all his company but five or six were killed. At an early hour next morning, the funeral party started for the home in Panola, where the body of the lamented young man, sacrificed to an unholy cause, was buried, at the close of the same day.

Louis Hughes, *Thirty Years a Slave: From Bondage to Freedom* (Milwaukee: South Side Printing Co., 1897), 117–19.

54

A SOUTHERN PUBLISHER ON THE CONSEQUENCES OF SURRENDER

J. B. D. De Bow founded De Bow's Review *in 1846. The influential publication initially focused on southern agricultural improvement. During the war it covered events from a pro-Confederate point of view. As Confederate armies dwindled, Union victory seemed terrifying to southerners, who despised their northern enemies and could not imagine a world without slavery.*

Our implacable, remorseless, and hated enemy has determined upon our *subjugation*. Will he achieve it? What is your answer? Are you willing, like the rebellious and truant school-boy, to be whipped back to the dominion and the tasks of a despot master? Has it occurred to you to meditate upon the full meaning of that word "subjugation?" The Austrian feels a tenderness for the Hungarian whom he has subjugated, the Turk may turn in pity from the Greeks he is about to smite, the Briton may raise up from the earth the enslaved Irishman, and the Cossack heel be lifted from the head of the Pole; but expect none of this mercy from a race who, trained by fanaticism to hatred of us in their schools and churches, preach a crusade of *extermination*. Read this in their papers, and see it illustrated in the course of their armies and their legislation. They would arm our slaves and preach domestic murder. Galled by the resistance they have met with, heated by their passions, excited by the hopes of plunder which conquest will give, long jealous of the prestige which the South enjoyed, desperate in their fortunes if deprived of [their] tribute, they were unwilling to enjoy under the restraints of the Constitution our fathers gave us—they brand us now as "traitors" and "rebels." . . . Could we face our wives and not blush to meet the faces of our little ones if, yielding the position of the master, we were willing to change places with our slaves? Ye, who are so solicitous of keeping together your odds and ends of property, dream not for a moment the Yankee master would suffer its enjoyment. He has threatened confiscation—he will carry it out. He is heaping up debt, and riotously expanding it, on the expectation that it will be shifted to your shoulders. Imagine the South subjugated, her people groaning under the debt of their own government. . . . Cunningly devised taxes will complete the work; and with the negroes liberated and left to roam in idleness and crime, or under despot rule, our fair land would become a hell indeed—a pandemonium more hideous than Milton's.

De Bow's Review, July 1864, vol. 34, old series, vol. 1, new series, 49–50.

55

AN EDITORIAL PRAISES THE RESTRAINT
OF BLACK SOLDIERS

The black-owned New Orleans Tribune *deplored a Confederate massacre of Union troops at Fort Pillow in Tennessee on April 12, 1864. While the exact sequence of events at Fort Pillow remains controversial, historians agree that Confederate soldiers under General Nathan Bedford Forrest killed scores of black troops after they had surrendered. The massacre was investigated by the U. S. Congress and widely denounced in the North. In contrast, the newspaper praised black troops for their more civilized behavior.*

It has also been said that the negroes take no prisoners, leaving it to be inferred that they remember [the massacre at] Fort Pillow, and are bent on having relentless retaliation. It is not so. I have made "stringent inquiry," and have yet to learn that they have in a single instance retaliated upon prisoners falling into their hands. On the contrary, General Banks informed me *that he saw two wounded colored soldiers helping a rebel wounded worse than they at the hospital.* It is evident, that the rebs think that they are to receive no mercy at the hands of the negroes. A guilty conscience needs no accuser. But how will it look in history—the barbarity on the one side, and the exhibition of forbearance, humanity, and Christianity on the other? Which will shine brighter? It is hard to wait for the coming years—for the time when such forbearance will be appreciated. When I read of Fort Pillow, I am ready for an exhibition of vigorous Christianity—a use of the bayonet; but who does not admire the leniency and mercy of the colored troops in contrast? Little do the rebel cotton lords, who have prided themselves on their plane of civilization, comprehend their position when set against that of their slaves, once but no longer—their damning shame—their barbarism now and forever held in abhorence. The colored men of America are making swift advance. The rebels are their best helpers just now—helping through their inhumanity.

I would not wish to have it understood that I think a negro better than a white man. God is the creator of all. They are men, and are now showing their manhood just as thousands of soldiers from New England and the whole North are doing. To make first rate soldiers they need discipline and instruction. To make good citizens they need education. They are receiving it. They have begun, and will go on. General South, commanding the 19th corps, speaks in high praise of their conduct. "They were subjected," said he, "to six hours' shell live, losing constantly, and they did not flinch. I was astounded at their good behavior." This is high praise, freely accorded.

Carleton

New Orleans Tribune, July 26, 1864.

56

THE TRANSITION FROM SLAVERY TO FREE LABOR IN THE MISSISSIPPI VALLEY

The New Orleans Tribune *was the only black-controlled newspaper in the Civil War South. The paper's roots lay in the free black community in New Orleans, which dated back to French control of the city before the Louisiana Purchase in 1804. In this article, the newspaper depicted life after slavery's demise in Union-controlled Louisiana.*

After a short time this so-called property enhanced so much in value, that [a] poor fellow was conveyed to the market, sold at private sale or bid off under the hammer of an auctioneer. Two young ones were then purchased, and brought home by the owner, who fattened them up and prepared them for the market. In the meantime, if the owner had nothing to occupy their time, they were hired at so much per month; the owner received the money as regularly as the month came round, and very often this monthly accumulation, was received more regularly than the rent of a public dwelling. By this means the slave-owners became rich, and indolence took the place of industry. Today the scene is somewhat changed. Slave labor is no longer recognized, and that man or woman, as the case may be, that was but a short time since held down by the yoke of oppression, is now at liberty to breathe the fresh air of heaven. No longer need they bow down in trembling worship to the master, nor will [they] fall prostrate by the lash of the steward at his command. No longer is public property recognized in man, and his daily and monthly accumulations are now his own, to be disposed of in any manner he may think best.

The liberty of this persecuted race has, it is true, been purchased at a dear rate. The blood of untold thousands has been poured out freely for the restoration of the Union, the liberty of the bondsman, and the promulgation of the dearly bought privileges of Jefferson. While our brave defenders march along fighting for a restored Union, the slaves are buckling on their armor, and take up their line of march in the same direction shouting for national liberty. The order of Gen. [Nathaniel] Banks, some time since, regulating slave labor has met with the happy approval of a great many of the friends of free labor. . . . The negro is compelled to work for Eight Dollars per month, that is provided he is a first-rate work hand. . . . Other classes of laborers get wages in accordance with the amount of work they can do. According to this, the condition of the slave is not materially altered. The Eight, Six, or Four dollars per month which they have the promise of getting from their employers, but which perhaps in a great many instances they may never receive, is scarcely enough to put an extra pair of boots upon their feet, say nothing of the hundred and one little incidental expenses, which are not embraced and could not be very well, in the existing contract. Already this subject receives considerable attention from men of different pursuits, and even is discussed through the columns of the Eastern press.

New Orleans Tribune, August 13, 1864.

57

A FORMER MISSISSIPPI SLAVE DESCRIBES
A FAILED ESCAPE ATTEMPT

Louis Hughes made several escape attempts during the war. After being moved by his master to Alabama in 1865, Hughes finally reached shelter behind Union lines. After the war, he worked as a nurse. Hughes himself paid to publish his autobiography. That arrangement gave Hughes full editorial control over the book's contents, making it especially valuable in the literature on slavery.

After I had been there three days, they started me back with letters for Boss. When I left it was near night, and I was to stop over at Master Jack's farm fifteen miles away. It was expected that I would reach Fryer's Point on the third morning, thus allowing me three days to go sixty miles; but I could not make much headway, as the roads were so heavy. The understanding was that I was to deliver the letters to the same gentleman, at Fryer's, to whom I delivered the others, for forwarding to Boss at Helena. I was then to go straight to the farm at Bolivar, and report to Smith, the overseer. But after I had got about four miles away, I concluded that I would not go back to the farm, but try to get to the Yankees. I knew I had disobeyed Smith by going down to the madam's to tell her about Boss, because he told me not to go when I spoke to him about it. And now if I went back I feared he would kill me; for I knew there would be no escape for me from being run into the bull ring, and that torture I could not think of enduring. I, therefore, stopped, and, taking the bridle and saddle from the horse, hid them in the corner of a fence in a cornfield. Then I went into the woods. The papers which I had were in the saddlebag safe. The place where I stayed in the daytime was a large shuck-pen—a pen built in the field to feed stock from, in the winter time. This pen was on Dr. Dandridge's farm; and the second night I worked my way up near the house. Knowing all the servants, I was watching a chance to send word to the coachman, Alfred Dandridge, that I wanted him to tell my wife that I was not gone. I went down to his cabin, in the quarters; and, after a short time he came. I was badly scared, and my heart was heavy and sore; but he spoke comfortingly to me, and I was cheered, somewhat, especially when he promised to see Matilda, and tell her of my whereabouts. He gave me some food, and hid me away for the night in his house. I kept close all the next day; and, at night, when all was still, Alfred and I crept out, and went to old Master Jack's. The distance was not great, and we soon covered it. Alfred went in and told my wife that I was outside and wanted to see her. She came out, and was so frightened and nervous that she commenced sobbing and crying, and almost fainted when I told her, in low tones, that I was going to try to get to Memphis, and that Alfred was helping me plan a way to this end. The rebels occupied both roads leading to Memphis, and I was puzzled to know how to reach the city without coming in contact with them. Two days after I had talked with my wife, the rebel troops who were camped on the Holly Springs road left for some other point. My friend Alfred found this out, and came and told me the encouraging news. The following night I went to old Master Jack's and told my wife that the way now seemed clear, and that I was going at once. I was bent on freedom, and would try for it again. I urged my wife not to grieve, and endeavored to encourage her by saying that I would return for her, as soon as possible, should I succeed in getting to a land [of] freedom. After many tears and blessings, we parted, and I left, Uncle Alfred going with me some three miles, as I was not acquainted with the road. When he left me I went on alone with gloomy forebodings, but resolved to do my best in this hazardous undertaking, whatever might happen. The road passed over hills and through swamps, and I found the traveling very wearisome. I had traveled some hours and thought I was doing well; when, about one o'clock in the night, I came out of a long swamp, and, reaching the top of a hill, I stopped for a moment's rest, raising myself to an erect position from that of walking, inclined by reason of weariness and the weight of saddle-bags thrown across my shoulders. The weather was bad, a heavy mist had come up, and it was so dark that I could hardly see my way. As I started on, a soldier yelled at me from the mist: "Halt! advance and give the countersign." I stopped immediately, almost scared out of my wits. "Come right up here," said the soldier, "or I'll blow you into eternity." I saw at once he was a rebel soldier. I knew not what to do. This place where I was halted was Nelson's farm, and the house was held as headquarters for a company of rebel soldiers, known as bushwhackers. While they belonged to the rebel army, they were, in a measure, independent of its regulations and discipline, kept back in the woods, ready for any depredation upon the property of union-ists—any outrage upon their persons. The soldier who had halted me took me up to the house, and all began to question me. I told them that I had been sent on an errand, and that I had lost my way. The next morning I was taken about a mile down in the swamp, over hills and through winding paths, till at last we came to the regular rebel camp. I was in great fear and thought my end had come. Here they began to question me again—the captain taking the lead; but I still stuck to my story that I had been sent on an errand, and had lost my way. I knew that this was my only chance. They tried to get me to say that I had come from the Yankees, as they were in camp near Holly Springs. They thought the Yankees had sent me out as a spy; but I said the same as at first—that I had lost my way. A soldier standing by said: "Oh! we will make you talk better than that"; and stepping back to his horse, he took a sea-grass halter, and said: "I'll hang you." There was a law or regulation of the rebel government directing or authorizing the hanging of any slave caught running away; and this fellow was going to carry it out to the letter. I talked and pleaded for my life. My feelings were indescribable. God only knows what they were. Dr. Carter, one of the soldiers, who knew me and the entire McGee family, spoke up and said: "You had better let me go and tell Mr. Jack McGee about him." The captain agreed to this, and the doc-tor went. The following day, Old Jack came, and steadily refused to consent to my being hung. He said: "I know Edmund would not have him hung. He is too valuable. No, no! we will put him in jail and feed him on bread and water—too valuable a nigger to be hung."

They tried again to make me say that I was with the Yankees. They whipped me a while, then questioned me again. The dog-wood switches that they used stung me terribly. They were commonly used in Mississippi for flogging slaves—one of the refinements of the cruelty of the institution of slavery. I refused to say anything different from what I had said; but when they had finished whipping me I was so sore I could hardly move. They made up their minds to put me in jail at Panola [Mississippi], twenty-two miles away, to be fed on bread and water. The next day was Sunday, and all arrangements having been made for taking me to the place appointed for those whose crime was a too great love for personal freedom, they started with me, passing on the way Old Master Jack's, where they halted to let him know that his advice respecting me was to be carried out. The old man called to my wife: "Come out and see Louis." Some one had told her that they were going to hang me; and I shall never forget her looks as she came out in the road to bid me good-by. One of the soldiers was softened by her agony, and whispered to her: "Don't cry, aunty, we are not going to hang him—we will only put him in jail." I saw this changed my wife's looks in a minute. I said a few words to her, and, with the prayer for God's blessing on us both, we parted, and they moved on. After we had gone about seven miles, we met two soldiers, who belonged to the regiment at Nelson. They said: "Hello! where you going with that nigger?" The two men in charge of me replied: "we are going to take him to Panola jail." "Why," said one of the soldiers, "there is no jail there; the Yanks passed through and pulled down the doors and windows of the jail, and let all the prisoners out." This caused a stop; and a council of war was held in the fence corner, the result of which was a decision to take me back to old Jack McGee's. After we had gotten back there, they took me and gave me another flogging to satisfy the madam. I was never so lacerated before. I could hardly walk, so sore and weak was I. The law was given me that if ever I was caught out in the public road again, by any soldier, I was to be shot. Monday morning I was sent to the field to plow; and, though I was very stiff and my flesh seemed sore to the bone, my skin drawn and shriveled as if dead, I had, at least, to make the attempt to work. To have said: "Master, I am too sore to work," would only have gotten me another whipping. So I obeyed without a word.

Louis Hughes, *Thirty Years a Slave: From Bondage to Freedom* (Milwaukee: South Side Printing Co., 1897), 129–37.

JEFFERSON DAVIS ADDRESSES THE PUBLIC

Some historians have criticized Jefferson Davis for failing to raise the morale of Confederate civilians. While he could not match Abraham Lincoln's eloquence, it was not for a lack of trying. Unlike Lincoln, he traveled around his country to bolster the enthusiasm of ordinary citizens. During a tour of the Confederacy in the winter of 1863–64 he gave the following speech in Columbia, South Carolina.

. . . Among those to whom we are indebted in South Carolina, I have not yet alluded to that peculiar claim of gratitude which is due to the fair countrywomen of the Palmetto State—they who have gone into the hospital to watch by the side of the sick—those who throng your way-side homes—who have nursed as if nursing was a profession—who have used their needle with the industry of sewing women—who have borne privation without a murmur and who have given up fathers, sons and husbands with more than Spartan virtue, because they called no one to witness and record the deed. Silently, with all the dignity and grandeur of patriotism, they have made their sacrifices—sacrifices which, if written, would be surpassed by nothing in history. If all the acts of heroism and virtue of the women of the South could be transmitted to the future, it would present such a record as the world has never seen. All honor, then, I say, to the ladies of the Palmetto State. Their gallantry is only different from that of her sons in this, that they deem it unfeminine to strike; and yet such is the heroism they have displayed—such the noble demeanor they have exhibited—that at the last moment, when trampled upon and it became a necessity, they would not hesitate to strike the invader a corpse at their feet. (Applause.)

. . . And with all sincerity, I say to my young friends here, if you want the right man for a husband, take him whose armless sleeve and noble heart betokens the duties that he has rendered to his country, rather than he who has never shared the toils, or borne the dangers of the field. If there still be left any of those military critics who have never spoken of our generals but to show how much better things could have been managed, or of our Government, but to find fault with it, because it never took their advice—in mercy's name, let these wise men go to the front and aid us in achieving our independence. With their wisdom and strength swelling our armies, I should have some hopes that I will not be a corpse before our cause is secured, and that our flag would never trail in dishonor, but would wave victoriously above the roar and smoke of battle.

I believe it is in the power of the men of the Confederacy to plant our banners on the banks of the Ohio, where we may say to the Yankee, "be quiet, or we will teach you another lesson." Within the next thirty days much is to be done, for upon our success much depends. Within the next thirty days, therefore, let all who are absentees, or who ought to be in the army, go promptly to their ranks. Let fresh victories crown our arms, and the peace party, if there be such at the North, can elect its candidate. But whether a peace candidate is elected or not, Yankee instinct will teach them that it is better to end the war and leave us to the enjoyment of our own rights.

Prayerful for your welfare, confiding in the army of the Confederate States to do that which soft words can never achieve, and in the hope that God will preserve the little ones of all brave men who are in the field, or who are going to it, and trusting that in the future, under brighter auspices, it may be my fortune to meet the good people of Columbia, I wish you all for the present farewell. (Applause.)

"Speech at Columbia," *Columbia (S.C.) Carolinian,* October 4, 1864, printed in *The Papers of Jefferson Davis,* vol. 11, ed. Linda Lasswell Crist (Baton Rouge: Louisiana State Univ. Press, 2003), 86–88.

1865

59

A TEXAS NEWSPAPER LACKS NEWS

After the Battle of Vicksburg in July 1863, the Union gained full control of the Mississippi River, which isolated Confederates in the vast area west of the Mississippi. Texas, Arkansas, and parts of Louisiana had little reliable information on the war's progress. This article appeared in a Galveston, Texas, newspaper. At that time, Galveston was the state's largest city and a crucial Confederate port. The paper's description of a major black rebellion at New Orleans's Fort Jackson was wishful thinking.

It will be observed that most of our late dispatches are from our enemies, and our readers do not need to be reminded that very little confidence can be placed in their statements. As another illustration of their systematic rule to falsity, so as to magnify their own exploits. It will be seen that they represent our forces at Fort Kaparensa, when it was abandoned in like manner, it is their uniform practice to represent our troops as suffering from want of clothing, food, &c, and as being utterly demoralized and anxious to terminate the war by unconditional submission. We know the facts to be precisely the reverse, that, as a general rule, our troops were never better clad and provided with food than at present, and never more determined to fight the Yankees as long as there is one left to pollute our soil. But these gross misrepresentations are all made to order, and for the accomplishment of an end. They know their dispatches are copied into our papers for the sake of the little truth that can be gleaned from them; and they expect that many of our people will be deceived by their false statements, and become discouraged and disheartened. By this means they expect to produce demoralization among our people by making them believe it exists in our army. While, therefore, we publish these dispatches, we would remind our readers that their only safe course will be to put down about one-half of them as gross falsehoods, while in the other truth there is, requires much care and labor in order to separate it from the exaggerations that are built upon it. . . .

It will be seen that the news we copy from the Telegraph to-day is more than usually interesting. The evidence of the negro insurrection in Fort Jackson seems to leave little room to doubt its correctness, although our late N. Orleans papers speak of it as quite a small affair, originating in a difficulty between some few of the negroes and a Federal officer. But even if true to the full extent now reported, showing that the negroes were successful in taking the Fort, destroying a steamer, &c., yet the negroes will, of course, be put down, and many of them made to suffer the death penalty.

There is no doubt that this revolt was owing to Yankee outrages upon them. This may be inferred from the notice of the affair in the New Orleans papers; and it is to be hoped that it may have some affect in opening the eyes of our negroes generally to the infamous deception practiced upon them by their pretended friends who are thus showing them-selves to be their worst enemies. We trust our negroes may be undeceived before it is too late, though many thousands of them are now suffering worse than death in Yankee hands, without any means of making their escape.

Galveston (Tex.) News, January 8, 1865.

60

CONFEDERATE EMANCIPATION
(THREE DOCUMENTS)

Robert E. Lee wrote this letter in response to an inquiry from Andrew Hunter, a member of the Virginia State Senate. In this dispatch, written less than three months before his Army of Northern Virginia surrendered to the Union, Lee belatedly recommended using black troops to fight for the Confederacy.

January 11, 1865
Hon. Andrew Hunter
Richmond, Va.:

Dear Sir:

I have received your letter of the 7th instant, and without confining myself to the order of your interrogatories, will endeavor to answer them by a statement of my views on the subject. I shall be most happy if I can contribute to the solution of a question in which I feel an interest commensurate with my desire for the welfare and happiness of our people.

Considering the relation of master and slave, controlled by humane laws and influenced by Christianity and an enlightened public sentiment, as the best that can exist between the white and black races while intermingled as at present in this country, I would deprecate any sudden disturbance of that relation unless it be necessary to avert a greater calamity to both. I should therefore prefer to rely upon our white population to preserve the ratio between our forces and those of the enemy, which experience has shown to be safe. But in view of the preparation of our enemies, it is our duty to provide for continued war and not for a battle or campaign, and I fear that we cannot accomplish this without overtaxing the capacity of our white population.

Should the war continue under the existing circumstances, the enemy may in course of time penetrate our country and get access to a large part of our negro population. It is his avowed policy to convert the able-bodied men among them into soldiers, and to emancipate all. The success of the Federal arms in the South was followed by a proclamation of President Lincoln for 280,000 men, the effect of which will be to stimulate the Northern States to procure as substitutes for their own people negroes thus brought within their reach. Many have already been obtained in Virginia, and should the fortune of war expose more of her territory, the enemy would gain a large accession to his strength. His progress will thus add to his numbers, and at the same time destroy slavery in a manner most pernicious to the welfare of our people. Their negroes will be used to hold them in subjection, leaving the remaining force of the enemy free to extend his conquest. Whatever may be the effect of our employing negro troops, it cannot be as mischievous as this. If it end in subverting slavery it will be accomplished by ourselves, and we can devise the means of alleviating the evil consequences to both races. I think, therefore, we must decide whether slavery shall be extinguished by our enemies and the slaves be used against us, or use them ourselves at the risk of the effects which must be produced upon our social institutions. My opinion is that we should employ them without delay. I believe that with proper regulations they can be made efficient soldiers. They possess the physical qualifications in an eminent degree. Long habits of obedience and subordination, coupled with the moral influence which in our country the white man possesses over the black, furnish an excellent foundation for that discipline which is the best guaranty of military efficiency. Our chief aim should be to secure their fidelity.

There have been formidable armies composed of men having no interest in the cause for which they fought beyond their pay and hope of plunder. But it is certain that the surest foundation upon which the fidelity of an army can rest, especially in a service which imposes peculiar hardships and privations, is the personal interest of the soldier in the issue of the contest. Such an interest we can give our negroes by giving immediate freedom to all who enlist, and freedom at the end of the war to the families of those who discharge their duties faithfully (whether they survive or not), together with the privilege of residing at the South. To this might be added a bounty for faithful service.

We should not expect slaves to fight for prospective freedom when they can secure it at once by going to the enemy, in whose service they will incur no greater risk than in ours. The reasons that induce me to recommend the employment of negro troops at all render the effect of the measures I have suggested upon slavery immaterial, and in my opinion the best means of securing the efficiency and fidelity of this auxiliary force would be to accompany the measure with a well-digested plan of gradual and general emancipation. As that will be the result of the continuance of the war, and will certainly occur if the enemy succeed, it seems to me most advisable to adopt it at once, and thereby obtain all the benefits that will accrue to our cause.

The employment of negro troops under regulations similar in principle to those above indicated would, in my opinion, greatly increase our military strength and enable us to relieve our white population to some extent. I think we could dispense with the reserve forces except in cases of necessity.

It would disappoint the hopes which our enemies base upon our exhaustion, deprive them in a great measure of the aid they now derive from black troops, and thus throw the burden of the war upon their own people. In addition to the great political advantages that would result to our cause from the adoption of a system of emancipation, it would exercise a salutary influence upon our whole negro population, by rendering more secure the fidelity of those who become soldiers, and diminishing the inducements to the rest to abscond.

I can only say in conclusion that whatever measures are to be adopted should be adopted at once. Every day's delay increases the difficulty. Much time will be required to organize and discipline the men, and action may be deferred until it is too late.

Very respectfully, your obedient servant,
R. E. Lee,
General

Robert E. Lee to Andrew Hunter, January 11, 1865, in *The War of the Rebellion: A Compilation of the Official Records of the Union and Confederate Armies* (Washington, D.C.: Government Printing Office, 1880–1901), series 1, vol. 52, part 2, 591.

Howell Cobb served as Speaker of the U. S. House of Representatives, as the governor of Georgia, and as a brigadier general in the South's Army of Northern Virginia. Even as Union troops under General William Tecumseh Sherman marched through his state, Cobb opposed even limited emancipation to strengthen the Confederate military.

HEADQRS. GEORGIA RESERVES AND MIL DIST OF GEORGIA.
Macon, Georgia, January 8, 1865
Hon. James A. Seddon,
Secretary of War, Richmond, Va.:

Sir:

. . . I think that the proposition to make soldiers of our slaves is the most pernicious idea that has been suggested since the war began. It is to me a source of deep mortification and regret to see that good and great man and soldier, General R.E. Lee, given as an authority for such a policy. My first hour of despondency will be the one in which that policy will be adopted. You cannot make soldiers of slaves, nor slaves of soldiers. The moment you resort to Negro soldiers your white soldiers will be lost to you; and one secret of the favor with which the proposition is received in portions of the Army is the hope that when negroes go into the army they [the white soldiers] will be permitted to retire. It is simply a proposition to fight the balance of the war with negro troops. You can't keep white and black troops together, and you can't trust negroes by themselves. It is difficult to get negroes enough for the purposes indicated in the President's message, much less enough for an army. Use all the negroes you can get, for all the purposes for which you need them, but don't arm them. The day you make soldiers of them is the beginning of the end of the revolution. If slaves will make good soldiers our whole theory of slavery is wrong—but they won't make good soldiers. As a class they are wanting in every qualification of a soldier. Better by far to yield to the demands of England and France to abolish slavery, and thereby purchase their aid, than resort to this policy, which is certain to lead to ruin and subjugation if it is adopted . . . at least try every reasonable mode of getting white solders. . . .

Sincerely, yours,
HOWELL COBB
Major-General

Howell Cobb to James A. Seddon, *The War of the Rebellion: A Compilation of the Official Records of the Union and Confederate Armies* (Washington, D.C.: Government Printing Office, 1880–1901), series 4, vol. 3, 1009–10.

––––––––––––

North Carolina publisher William Woods Holden discussed the idea of Confederate emancipation of slaves who served as soldiers. Holden's assertion that black troops would receive a homestead after the war seems to be unsupported by written evidence.

It is Lincoln doctrine. It is the very doctrine which the war was commenced to put down. Surely we ought to have peace now, since the extremes have met, since the partizans of Mr. Lincoln and the partizans of Mr. Davis have united in the advocacy of abolition, but they are to have their freedom and a *homestead* at the end of the war, as their reward! The Negro soldier is to have a homestead, but the white soldier is promised nothing!—No homestead is provided for him. His wife and children, already beggared by the war, must toil on, and the children must grow up in ignorance and rags, because he is white; but the *negro* is to have his freedom and a *homestead*. The negro is to be the pet, and the gallant white veteran, with the scars of fifty battles on his body, is to be turned off to work as a tenant, if he has no land, and must be jostled and insulted in his neighborhood as long as he lives, by his black comrade, who is to have a homestead provided for him by the State! If this is not *negrophobia* run mad, we know not what it is. Why, our enemies have not yet proposed to divide our land among the negroes. Aggressive and harsh as they are, they have appeared disposed thus far to have spared us this humiliation. . . . It is apparent that we are rapidly approaching that point in our progress which will involve us, unless some check is interposed, in all the horrors of the French Revolution. The two sections are vieing with each other in the work of emancipation. The negroes are to be armed and society is to be not merely upset, but destroyed—We call upon the Legislature of this State, now in session, to rise to the magnitude of the occasion, and not only to stamp this infamous proposition with the seal of its reprobation, but to adopt promptly the most vigorous measures to ensure an honorable PEACE, which can alone close this Pandora's box of ills untold, and put us again in the enjoyment of prosperity, freedom, and happiness.

North Carolina Weekly Standard, January 18, 1865.

61

A SOUTH CAROLINA WRITER DESCRIBES
THE BURNING OF COLUMBIA

Before the Civil War, South Carolina's William Gilmore Simms had a
successful career writing historical fiction. During the war, the pro-
slavery author produced newspaper accounts of life in his state. Simms
blamed General William T. Sherman for the burning of Columbia,
South Carolina, in February 1865. In response, Sherman denied re-
sponsibility for the inferno. His defenders argued that it was impos-
sible to fault one individual for the fire. Instead, they blamed a volatile
combination of young soldiers, strong winds, drunkenness, and a
highly flammable commodity, cotton.

. . . We had heard of some few outrages, or attempts at outrages,
of the worst sort, but the instances, in the case of the white females,
must have been very few. There was, perhaps, a wholesome dread
of goading to desperation the people whom they had despoiled of all
but honor. They could see, in many watchful and guardian eyes, the
lurking expression which threatened sharp vengeance, should their
trespasses proceed to those extremes which they yet unquestionably
contemplated.

And yet, we should grossly err if, while showing the forbearance
of the soldiers in respect to the *white* women, we should convey to
any reader the notion that they exhibited a like forbearance in the
case of the *black*. The poor Negroes were terribly victimized by their
assailants, many of them besides the instances mentioned being
left in a condition a little short of death. Regiments, in successive
relays, subjected scores of these poor women to the torture of their
embraces, and—but we dare not further pursue the subject. There

are some horrors that the historian dare not pursue—which the painter dare not delineate. They let drop the curtains over crimes which humanity bleeds to contemplate.

The "pluck" of our women was especially a subject of acknowledgment. They [Union soldiers] could admire a quality with which they had not soul to sympathize—or rather the paramount passion for greed and plunder—in subjection all other qualities, without absolutely extinguishing them from their minds and thoughts. To inspire terror in the weak, strange to say, seemed to them a sort of heroism. To extort fear and awe appeared to their inordinate vanity a tribute more grateful than any other, and a curious conflict was sometimes carried on in their minds between their vanity and cupidity.

[Dr. Sill], an esteemed and well-known citizen of Columbia, writes as follows:

"On Thursday, the day before the evacuation of the Confederate forces, I invited a very poor French lady, Madame Pelletier, with her child, refugees from Charleston, to take shelter where they might, at least, have such protection as I could give her, shelter and food—for herself and child. She was poor, indeed, having very little clothing, and only one or two implements—a sewing machine and a crimping apparatus—by means of which she obtained a precarious support. My own family (happily) and servants being all absent, and being myself incapacitated by years of sickness from making any exertion, all that the poor widow woman and myself could remove from the house, besides a few things of hers, consisted of two bags of flour, a peck of meal, and about the same of grist, and about thirty pounds of bacon and a little sugar. These few things we managed to get out of the house, and by the aid of a wheelbarrow, removed about fifty yards from the burning buildings. Waiting then and there, waiting anxiously the progress and direction of the fire, we soon found that we had been robbed of one bag of flour and a trunk of valuable books of account and papers. The fire continued to advance on us, we found it necessary to remove again. About this time, there came up a stalwart soldier, about six feet high, accoutered with pistols, Bowie-knife, &c., and stooping down over the remaining bag of flour, demanded of the poor French lady what the bag contained. Having lost, but a few moments before, almost everything she had in the way of provisions, she seemed most deeply and keenly alive to her destitute situation, in the event she should lose the remaining bag of flour; the last and only hope of escape from starvation of her child and herself. She fell upon her knees, with hands uplifted, in a supplicating manner, and most piteously and imploringly set forth her situation—an appeal which, under the circumstances, it would be impossible to conceive, more touching or heart-rending. She told him she was not here of her own choice; that herself and husband had come to Charleston in 1860 to better their fortunes, that they had been domiciled in New Jersey, where her husband had taken the necessary steps to become a citizen of the United States. She had in her hand his papers vouching the truth of her statement; that her husband had died of yellow fever in Charleston; that being unable, from want of means to return to New Jersey, she had been driven from Charleston to Columbia, (a refugee, flying from the enemy's shells,) to try to make an honest support for herself and child. To all this, he not only turned a deaf ear, but deliberately drew from his breast a huge shining Bowie-knife, brandished it in her face, rudely pushed her aside, using, at the same time, the most menacing and obscene language; shouldered the bag of flour, and marched off, leaving the poor starving creature, with her helpless child, overwhelmed with grief and despair."

E. SILL.

This surely is very piteous to hear, and were the case an isolated one, it would probably move compassion in every heart; but where the miseries of [the] worst sort, of a whole community of twenty thousand, amassed, as it were, together before the eyes, the sensibilities become obtuse, and the universal suffering seems to destroy the sensibilities in all. We shall not seek to multiply instances like the foregoing, which would be an endless work and to little profit.

William Gilmore Simms, *The Sack and Destruction of the City of Columbia, S.C.* (Columbia: Power Press of the Daily Phoenix, 1865), 29–30.

62

A FORMER SLAVE REMEMBERS EMANCIPATION

Malindy Maxwell shared her recollections of slavery's demise with an interviewer from the Work Projects Administration. While her language is understated, she provides insight into the experiences of both blacks and whites.

Interviewer Miss Irene Robertson
Person Interviewed: Malindy Maxwell; Madison, Arkansas.
Age: Up in 80's

"I was born close to Como and Bardis, Mississippi. My master and mistress were Sam Shans and Miss Cornelia Shans. They owned ma and Master Rube Sanders owned pa. Neither owner would sell but they agreed to let ma and pa marry. . . .

"I don't know how old I am but I was a good size girl when emancipation came. Miss Cornelia had my age in her Bible. They took me from the cabin and I was staying at the house. I slept on a trundle bed under Miss Cornelia's bed. Her bed was a toaster—way high up, had a big stool to step on to go up there and she had it curtained off. I had a good cotton bed and I slept good up under there. Her bed was corded with a sea grass rope.

"I recollect a right smart of the Civil War. We were close enough to hear the roar and rumble and the big cannons shake the things in the house. I don't know where they were fighting—a long ways off I guess.

"I saw the soldiers scouting. They came most any time. They went in and took every drop of milk out of the churn. They took anything they could find and went away with it. I saw the cavalry come through. I thought they looked so pretty. Their canteens were shining in the sun. Miss Cornelia told me to hide, the soldiers might take me on with them. I didn't want to go. I was very well pleased there at Miss Cornelia's.

"I saw the cavalry come through that raised the 'white sheet.' I know now it must have been a white flag but they called it a white sheet to quit fighting. It was raised a short time after they passed and they said they was the ones raised it. I don't know where it was. I reckon it was a big white flag they raised up. It was so they could stop fighting.

"Mars Sam Shan didn't go to the war; he hid out. He said it was a useless war, he wasn't going to get shot up for no use at all, and he never went a step. He hid out. I don't know where. I know Charles would take the baskets off. Charles tended to the stock and the carriage. He drove the wagon and carriage. He fetched water and wood. He was a black boy. Mars Sam Shan said he wasn't going to lose his life for nothing.

"Miss Cornelia would cook light corn bread and muffins and anything also they had to cook. Rations got down mighty scarce before it was done with. They put the big round basket nearly big as a split cotton basket out on the back portico. Charles come and disappeared with it.

"Chess and Charles were colored overseers. We didn't have white overseers. Miss Cornelia and Miss Chloe would walk the floor and cry and I would walk between. I would cry feeling sorry for them, but I didn't know why they cried so much. I know it was squally times. War is horrible.

"Mars Sam Shan came home, went down to the cabins—they was scattered over the fields—and told them the War was over, they was free but that they could stay. Then come some runners, white men. They were Yankee men. I know that now. They say you must get pay or go off. We stayed that year. Another man went to pa and said he would give him half of what he made. He got us all up and we went to Pleasant Hill. We did tolerably well. . . ."

Slave Narratives: A Folk History of Slavery in the United States From Interviews with Former Slaves, vol. 2, *Arkansas Narratives,* part 5, Typewritten Records Prepared by the Federal Writers' Project, Work Projects Administration for the District of Columbia, Sponsored by the Library of Congress (Washington, D.C.: Work Projects Administration, 1941), 57–63, available online at "Born in Slavery: Slave Narratives from the Federal Writer's Project, 1936–1938," https://memory.loc.gov/ammem/snhtml/mesnbibVolumes1.html.

63

A WHITE OFFICER DESCRIBES FREEDMEN WHO
FOUGHT IN THE UNION ARMY

Thomas Wentworth Higginson, an author and Unitarian minister, helped lead the abolitionist movement in the 1850s. He took part in mob actions designed to free captive runaways in New England and supplied weapons to antislavery settlers in Kansas. In 1862, he led the 1st South Carolina Volunteers, one of the initial Union regiments made up of former slaves.

So far as I have seen, the mass of men are naturally courageous up to a certain point. A man seldom runs away from danger which he ought to face, unless others run; each is apt to keep with the mass, and colored soldiers have more than the usual of this gregariousness. In almost every regiment, black or white, there are a score or two of men who are naturally daring, who really hunger after dangerous adventures, and are happiest when allowed to seek them. Every commander gradually finds out who these men are, and habitually uses them; certainly I had such, and I remember with delight their bearing, their coolness, and their dash. Some of them were negroes, some mulattos. One of them would have passed for white, with brown hair and blue eyes, while others were so black you could hardly see their features. These picked men . . . had the two-o'clock-in-the-morning courage, which Napoleon thought so rare. The mass of the regiment rose to the same level under excitement, and were more excitable, I think, than whites, but neither more nor less courageous. . . .

There was a family named Wilson, I remember, of which we had several representatives. Three or four brothers had planned an escape from the interior to our lines; they finally decided that the youngest should stay and take care of the old mother; the rest, with their sister and her children, came in a "dug-out" down one of the rivers. They were fired upon, again and again, by the pickets along the banks, until finally every man on board was wounded; and still they got safely through. When the bullets began to fly about them, the woman shed tears, and her little girl of nine said to her, "Don't cry mother, Jesus will help you," and then the child began praying as the wounded men still urged the boat along. This the mother told me, but I had previously heard it from an officer who was on the gunboat that picked them up,—a big, rough man, whose voice fairly broke as he described their appearance. He said that the mother and child had been hid for nine months in the woods before attempting their escape, and the child would speak to no one,—indeed, she hardly would when she came to our camp. . . ."

There was another family of brothers in the regiment named Miller. Their grandmother, a fine-looking old woman, nearly seventy, I should think, but erect as a pine-tree, used sometimes to come and visit them. She and her husband had once tried to escape from a plantation near Savannah. They had failed, and had been brought back; the husband had received five hundred lashes, and while the white men on the plantation were viewing the punishment, she was collecting her children and grandchildren, to the number of twenty-two, in a neighboring marsh, preparatory to another attempt that night. They found a flat-boat which had been rejected as unseaworthy, got on board,—still under the old woman's orders,—and drifted forty miles down the river to our lines. Trowbridge happened to be on board the gunboat which picked them up, and he said that when the "flat" touched the side of the vessel, the grandmother rose to her full height, with her youngest grandchild in her arms, and said only, "My God! are we free?" By one of those coincidences of which life is full, her husband escaped also, after his punishment, and was taken up by the same gunboat.

Thomas Wentworth Higginson, *Army Life in a Black Regiment by Thomas Wentworth Higginson, Late Colonel 1st South Carolina Volunteers* (Boston: Fields, Osgood, and Co., 1870), 244–48.

64

"HOW FREEDOM CAME"

In this interview with the Works Progress Administration, Robert Farmer reflected on gaining his freedom. He was about twelve years old in 1865. He recalled an uncertain path from slavery to free labor.

Interviewer: Samuel S. Taylor
Robert Farmer
1612 Battery Street, Little Rock, Arkansas
Age: 84

"My father's master was Isaac Farmer. My mother didn't belong to him. She belonged to the Sharpes. Just what her master's name was I don't recollect. She lived five miles from my father. He went to see her every Thursday night. That was his regular night to go. He would go Saturday night; if you went any other time and the patrols could catch him, they would whip him just the same as though he belonged to them. But they never did whip my father because they never could catch him. He was one of those who ran.

"My father and mother had ten children. I don't know whether any of them is living now or not besides myself. . . ."

HOW FREEDOM CAME

"Freedom was a singsong every which way when I knowed anything. My father's master, Isaac Farmer, had a big farm and a whole world of land. He told the slaves all of them were free. He told his brother's slaves, 'After you have made this crop, bring your wives and children here because I am able to take care of them.' He had a smokehouse full of meat and other things. He told my father that after this crop is gathered, to fetch his wife and children to him [Isaac Farmer], because Sharpe might not be able to feed and shelter and take care of them all. So my father brought us up to Isaac Farmer's farm.

"I never did anything but devilment the whole second year of freedom. I was large enough to take water in the field but I didn't have to do that. There were so many of them there that one could do what he pleased. The next year I worked because they had thinned out. The first year came during this surrender. They cared for Sharpe's crop. The next year they took Isaac Farmer's invitation and stayed with him. The third year many of them went other places, but my father and my mother and brothers and sisters stayed with Isaac Farmer for a while. . . .

"My mother used to milk and I used to rope the calves and hold them so that they couldn't get to the cow. I had to keep the horses in the canebrake so they could eat. That was to keep the soldiers from getting a fine black horse the master had. . . ."

SOLDIERS

"But they got him just the same. The Yankees used to come in blue uniforms and some right on in without asking anything. They would take your horse and ask nothing. They would go into the smokehouse and take out shoulders, hams, and side meat, and they would take all the wine and brandy that was there. . . ."

DANCES AFTER FREEDOM

"Two sisters stayed in North Carolina in a two-room house in Wilson County. There was a big drove of us and we all went to town in the evening to get whiskey. There was one man who had a wife with us, but all the rest were single. We cut the pigeon wing, waltzed, and quadrilled. We danced all night until we burned up all the wood. Then we went down into the swamp and brought back each one as long a log as he could carry. We chopped this up and piled it in the room. Then we went on across the swamp to another plantation and danced there.

"When we got through dancing, I looked at my feet and the bottom of them was plumb naked. I had just bought new boots, and had danced the bottoms clean out of them. . . .

Slave Narratives: A Folk History of Slavery in the United States From Interviews with Former Slaves, vol. 2, *Arkansas Narratives,* part 2, Typewritten Records Prepared by the Federal Writers' Project, Work Projects Administration for the District of Columbia, Sponsored by the Library of Congress (Washington, D.C.: Work Projects Administration, 1941), 271–75, available online at "Born in Slavery: Slave Narratives from the Federal Writer's Project, 1936–1938," https://memory.loc.gov/ammem/snhtml/mesnbib Volumes1.html.

BOOKER T. WASHINGTON RECALLS SLAVERY
AND FREEDOM

Booker T. Washington was born into slavery in 1856. After slavery, he became an educator and the leading spokesman for black Americans in the late nineteenth and early twentieth centuries. Based at a vocational college, the Tuskegee Institute in Alabama, he sought compromise and economic cooperation with whites at a time when segregation and lynching became increasingly pervasive across the South. Washington's book Up from Slavery *captures his spirit of restrained optimism. While his language was circumspect, he provided an eloquent condemnation of slavery.*

I was asked not long ago to tell something about the sports and pastimes that I engaged in during my youth. Until that question was asked it had never occurred to me that there was no period of my life that was devoted to play. From the time that I can remember anything, almost every day of my life has been occupied in some kind of labour; though I think I would now be a more useful man if I had had time for sports. During the period that I spent in slavery I was not large enough to be of much service, still I was occupied most of the time in cleaning the yards, carrying water to the men in the fields, or going to the mill, to which I used to take the corn, once a week, to be ground. The mill was about three miles from the plantation. This work I always dreaded. The heavy bag of corn would be thrown across the back of the horse, and the corn divided about evenly on each side; but in some way, almost without exception, on these trips, the corn would so shift as to become unbalanced and would fall off the horse, and often I would fall with it. As I was not strong enough to reload the corn upon the horse, I would have to wait, sometimes for many hours, till a chance passer-by came along who would help me out of my trouble. The hours while waiting for some one were usually spent crying. The time consumed in this way made me late in reaching the mill, and by the time I got my corn ground and reached home it would be far into the night. The road was a lonely one, and often led through dense forests. I was always frightened. The woods were said to be full of soldiers who had deserted from the army, and I had been told that the first thing a deserter did to a Negro boy when he found him alone was to cut off his ears. Besides, when I was late in getting home I knew I would always get a severe scolding or a flogging.

During the campaign when Lincoln was first a candidate for the Presidency, the slaves on our far-off plantation, miles from any railroad or large city or daily newspaper, knew what the issues involved were. When war was begun between the North and the South, every slave on our plantation felt and knew that, though other issues were discussed, the primal one was that of slavery. Even the most ignorant members of my race on the remote plantations felt in their hearts with a certainty that admitted of no doubt, that freedom of the slaves would be the one great result of the war, if the Northern armies conquered. Every success of the Federal armies and every defeat of the Confederate forces was watched with the keenest and most intense interest. Often the slaves got knowledge of the results of great battles before the white people received it. This news was usually gotten from the colored man who was sent to the post-office for the mail. In our case the post-office was about three miles from the plantation, and the mail came once or twice a week. The man who was sent to the office would linger about the place long enough to get the drift of the conversation from the group of white people who naturally congregated there, after receiving their mail, to discuss the latest news. The mail-carrier on his way back to our master's house would as naturally retell the news that he had secured among the slaves, and in this way they often heard of important events before the white people at the "big house," as the master's house was called.

I cannot remember a single instance during my childhood or early boyhood when our entire family sat down to the table together, and

God's blessing was asked, and the family ate a meal in a civilized manner. On the plantation in Virginia, and even later, meals were gotten by the children very much as dumb animals get theirs. It was a piece of bread here and a scrap of meat there. It was a cup of milk at one time and some potatoes at another. Sometimes a portion of our family would eat out of the skillet or pot, while some one else would eat from a tin plate held on the knees, and often using nothing but the hands with which to hold the food. When I had grown to sufficient size, I was required to go to the "big house" at meal-times to fan the flies from the table by means of a large set of paper fans operated by a pulley. Naturally much of the conversation of the white people turned upon the subject of freedom and the war, and I absorbed a good deal of it. I remember that at one time I saw two of my young mistresses and some lady visitors eating ginger-cakes, in the yard. At that time those cakes seemed to me to be absolutely the most tempting and desirable things that I had ever seen; and I then and there resolved that, if I ever got free, the height of my ambition would be reached if I could get to the point where I could secure and eat ginger-cakes in the way that I saw those ladies doing.

Of course as the war was prolonged the white people, in many cases, often found it difficult to secure food for themselves. I think the slaves felt the deprivation less than the whites, because the usual diet for the slaves was corn bread and pork, and these could be raised on the plantation; but coffee, tea, sugar, and other articles which the whites had been accustomed to use could not be raised on the plantation, and the conditions brought about by the war frequently made it impossible to secure these things. The whites were often in great straits. Parched corn was used for coffee, and a kind of black molasses was used instead of sugar. Many times nothing was used to sweeten the so-called tea and coffee. . . .

Finally the war closed, and the day of freedom came. It was a momentous and eventful day to all upon our plantation. We had been expecting it for months. Deserting soldiers returning to their homes were to be seen every day. Others who had been discharged, or whose regiments had been paroled, were constantly passing near our place. The "grape-vine telegraph" was kept busy night and day. The news and mutterings of great events were swiftly carried from one plantation to another. In the fear of "Yankee" invasions, the silverware and other valuables were taken from the "big house," buried in the woods, and guarded by trusted slaves. Woe be to any one who would have attempted to disturb the buried treasure. The slaves would give the Yankee soldiers food, drink, clothing—anything but that which had been specifically entrusted to their care and honor. As the great day drew nearer, there was more singing in the slave quarters than usual. It was bolder, had more ring, and lasted later into the night. Most of the verses of the plantation songs had some reference to freedom.

Booker T. Washington, *Up from Slavery: An Autobiography* (New York: Doubleday, Page and Co., 1907), 5–12.

——— 66 ———

"MY UNMITIGATED HATRED TO YANKEE RULE":
EDMUND RUFFIN'S SUICIDE

The surrender of Confederate armies in April 1865 left Edmund Ruffin, the proslavery radical who fired the first shot in the war, in despair. In June 1865 he wrote a long and rambling suicide note, part of which appears below. Ruffin's note captures his despondence when the Confederacy lost the war. He could scarcely imagine his world without slavery. Ruffin emphatically closed the note with "The End."

June 16, 1865 [June 16–18, 1865]

... In addition, there were some matters of public importance, after the surrender of Gen. Lee's army, which I desired to know the end of. Among these were the fortunes of the army under Gen. [Joseph] Johnston, & whether our struggle against Yankee domination & despotism might still, & would, be continued west of the Mississippi. ... And I was not unwilling to delay for more trivial causes, if they were capable of adding some interest to my passing days, & especially while there yet was no doubt of my ultimate determination. I was willing to allow full time for my mind to be given a different direction. But up to this time, [the 18th], the longer I have thought on the subject, the more have my first doubts & fears been lessened, & the more decided have I become as to the necessity for my designed course. So far as I can now foresee, I have little now to do except to add some directions in writing.

I here declare my unmitigated hatred to Yankee rule—to all political, social & business connections with Yankees—& to the Yankee race. Would that I could impress these sentiments, in their full force, on every living southerner, & bequeath them to every one yet to be born! May such sentiments be held universally in the outraged & down-trodden South, though in silence & stillness, until the now far-distant day shall arrive for just retribution for Yankee usurpation, oppression, & atrocious outrages & for deliverance & vengeance for the now ruined, subjugated, & enslaved Southern States! May the maledictions of every victim to their malignity, press with full weight on the perfidious Yankee people & their perjured rulers—& especially on those of the invading forces who perpetrated, & their leaders & higher authorities who encouraged, directed, or permitted, the unprecedented & generally extended outrages of robbery, rapine & destruction, & house-burning, all committed contrary to the laws of war on non-combatant residents, & still worse on aged men & helpless women!

Edmund Ruffin sen.
Redmoor, 10 A. M., June 18th 1865

THE END

William Kauffman Scarborough, ed., *The Diary of Edmund Ruffin,* vol. 3, *A Dream Shattered, June 1863–June 1865* (Baton Rouge: Louisiana State Univ. Press, 1989), 945–46.

ACKNOWLEDGMENTS

This project has benefited from the help of many people. Joe Danielson read the entire manuscript and provided wise counsel. An undergraduate, Emily Berns, found an especially intriguing document, while graduate assistant John Williams helped with proofreading and double-checking source material. Over the years, I have been especially aided by the intellectual stimulation and practical support of Bob Martin, Don Shepherdson, Jim Oakes, Greg Bruess, Ken Lyftogt, Julie Husband, Nancy Isenberg, Barbara Cutter, Brian Roberts, Nancy MacLean, Jim O'Loughlin, Andy Burstein, Tom Connors, Lou Fenech, and the late John Baskerville.

I am grateful for the libraries of the University of Iowa and the University of Northern Iowa. I especially appreciate Rosemary Meany and UNI's Interlibrary Loan Department. Thanks go to the University of Virginia for its Special Collections Library and Valley of the Shadow Project, the Library of Congress, and the libraries of the Virginia Military Institute, Washington and Lee University, and the University of South Carolina. The University of North Carolina's Documenting the American South Collection has also been valuable.

The University of Northern Iowa provided a leave and summer research support as I began to work on this book. Rand Dotson of the Louisiana State University Press has been helpful in moving the project forward.

This book is dedicated to Arlo Hettle in appreciation of his sense of humor, which helps get me through the day. I cannot imagine a more supportive partner than Leslie Cohn. I would say more about Leslie, but words fail me.

INDEX

African Americans: abolitionists, black, 66–68; education of, 66–68; *New Orleans Bee* on management of black labor, 88–89; soldiers, black, 153–56, 157–58, 169–70, 185–90, 197–98
Alabama, 124–25
Anderson, Robert, xi
anti-Semitism, 96–98
Army Life in a Black Regiment (Higginson), 197–98
Atkinson, Rev. Thomas D. D., 29–31
Augusta Constitutionalist, 86–87
autobiographies, 6–9, 20–21, 40–41. *See also* diaries; memoirs

Bartow, Francis S., 33
Battle Cry of Freedom (McPherson), xvi
battle flag, Confederate, xvii
Beauregard, Pierre G. T., 33
Bell, John, 6
A Belle of the Fifties (Clay-Clopton), 124–25
black abolitionists, 66–68
black soldiers, 153–56, 157–58, 169–70, 185–90, 197–98
Bond, Priscilla, 147
bread riot, Richmond, VA, 99–105
Breckinridge, John C., 54
Brokenburn: The Journal of Kate Stone (Anderson, ed.), 53–55, 106–10
Brown, Joseph, 59–60, 121–23
Brown, William Wells, 79–83

Brownlow, William G. "Parson," 56–58
Butler, Benjamin F., 22–25, 84–85, 88

Campbell, John Archibald, 101
Carrington, Abram C., 73–75
Carroll, William Henry, 58
Charleston, NC, xi, 13–15
Chase, Salmon P., xii
Chesnut, James, Jr., 51–52
"Christian Duty in the Present Time of Trouble" (Atkinson), 29–31
Christian Intelligencer, 99–100
"The Christian Soldier" (Dabney), 73–75
Civil War: first shot fired in, xi, 13–15; "hard war" tactics, Union, 145–46; "Lost Cause" theory, xv; surrender, xi–xii, 167–68, 206. *See also specific persons and topics*
Clay, Clement Claiborne, 124–25
Clay-Clopton, Virginia, 124–25
Cleburne, Patrick, 153–56
Co. Aytch (Watkins), 159–62
Cobb, Howell, 188–89
Colston, Raleigh T., 62, 151–52
Columbia, SC, 178–79, 191–93
conscription, 51–52, 59–60, 121–23
"Cornerstone" speech (Stephens), 10–12
Cox, Oliver M., 131–34
Crudemp, Minger, 20

Dabney, Robert Lewis, 73–75
Davenport, Jo. D. L., 18–19

Davis, Jefferson, 59–60, 121, 131–34, 142–44, 163–64, 178–79
Days of Bondage (Jones), 20–21
De Bow's Review, 167–68
diaries: Bond, 147; Brownlow, 56–58; Holmes, 113–15; Jones, 64–65, 100–102; McGuire, 61–63, 150–51; Ruffin, 13–15, 206–7; Stone, 53–55, 106–10; Tillson, 140–41; Waddell, 93–95; Williamson, 119–20. *See also* memoirs
Diary of a Southern Refugee (McGuire), 61–63, 151–52
Diary of Edmund Ruffin (Ruffin, ed. Scarborough), xi–xii, 13–15, 206–7
The Diary of Miss Emma Holmes (Holmes, ed. Marszalek), 113–15
Dodge, Grenville, 145
Douglas, Stephen, 6
draft, Confederate, 51–52, 59–60, 121–23
Duvel, John W., 116

education of African Americans, 66–68
Elzey, Arnold, 102, 105
emancipation, xii, 185–90, 194–96, 199–201

Farmer, Robert, 199–201
Farthing, Paul, 138–39
Fitzgerald, William, 128–30
Foote, Shelby, xv
Forrest, Nathan Bedford, 169
Forten, Charlotte, 66–68
Fort Jackson, LA, 183–84
Fort Monroe, VA, 22–25
Fort Pillow, TN, 169–70
Fort Sumpter, SC, x, 13–15, 26, 82
Freeman, Douglas Southall, xv

Galveston News, 183–84
Gettysburg Address, xv
Glasgow, Francis T., 42–44
Golladay, Edward, 57–58
Grandy, Charles, 49–50

Grant, Ulysses S., 145, 157
Gwynne, Julia P., 137–38

Hammond, Harry, 45–46
Hammond, James Henry, 45–46
Hannah, Samuel B., 111–12
"hard war" tactics, Union, 145–46
Haun, C. A., 57
Higginson, Thomas Wentworth, 197–98
Hines, Howell, 16–18
The History of William Webb, Composed by Himself (Webb), 6–9
Hoggard, David, 49
Holden, William Woods, 26–28, 189–90
Holmes, Emma, 113–15
horses, stolen, 118
Hughes, Louis, 165–66, 173–77
Hunter, Andrew, 185–88

Jackson, Mattie J., 40–41
Jackson, Thomas "Stonewall," xv, 61–62, 73, 111–12
Jefferson, Thomas, 11
"The Jews and the War" (*Richmond Examiner*), 96–98
Johnson, Andrew, 69–72
Jones, Friday, 20–21
Jones, John B., 64–65, 100–102, 163–64
Jordan, S. P., 117

King, Martin Luther, Jr., xvi

Lee, Robert E., xi–xii, xv, 61–62, 185–88, 206
Lenoir, Walter, 135–39
Letcher, John, 101, 105
letters: Brown, 59–60; Chesnut, 51–52; Cleburne, 153–56; Cobb, 188–89; to Davis, 131–34, 142–44; Fitzgerald to Lincoln, 128–30; Glasgow, 42–44; Hammond, 45–46; Hannah, 111–12; to Pettus, 16–19
The Liberator, 66–68

Lincoln, Abraham: Confederate views of, 6–7, 26, 135, 186, 189; Davis compared to, 178; Gettysburg Address, xv; letters to, 128–30; in slave accounts, 21; Stephens and, 10
Logan, John A., 145–46
Longstreet, James, 33
"Lost Cause" theory, xv

Mallory, Charles K., 22–24
"Mammy" figure, 76–78, 104
A Maryland Bride in the Deep South (Bond, ed. Harrison), 147
Maxwell, Malindy, 194–96
McClellan, George, 62–63
McGee, Mack, 165–66
McGuire, Judith W., 61–63, 151–52
McPherson, James, xvi
Melvin, Robert, 131–34
memoirs: Clay-Clopton, 124–25; Harrison, 32–34; Pryor, 104–5; Watkins, 159–62. *See also* diaries; slave narratives and accounts
Memphis freedmen's resolutions, 157–58
ministers, 29–31, 73–75
Mississippi Declaration of secession, 3–5
Mosby's Rangers (Williamson), 119–20

Natchez Daily Courier, 126–27
New Orleans Bee, 88–89
New Orleans Tribune, 169–70, 171–72
newspapers, journals, and magazines: *Augusta Constitutionalist* on "faithful" slave, 86–87; *Christian Intelligencer* on price gouging, 99–100; *De Bow's Review* on consequences of surrender, 167–68; *Galveston News* and lack of news, 183–84; *Natchez Daily Courier* on masters and slaves, 126–27; *New Orleans Bee* on Union management of black labor, 88–89; *New Orleans Tribune* on black soldiers, 169–70;

North Carolina Weekly Standard on secession, 26–28; "The Private History of a Campaign that Failed" (Twain), *Century Magazine,* 35–39; *Richmond Examiner* letter to the editor on Jews, 96–98
North Carolina Weekly Standard, 26–28, 189–90
Norwood, Joseph C., 138–39

Paducah, Kentucky, 7–8
Pettus, John J., 16–19
Planter (steamship), 79–83
poetry, 76–78
prisons and prisoners, 56–58, 64–65, 69–70, 128–30, 140–41
"The Private History of a Campaign that Failed" (Twain), 35–39
Pryor, Sara Agnes Rice, 104–5

Randolph, G. W., 51–52
A Rebel War Clark's Diary (Jones), 64–65, 100–102
Refugitta of Richmond (Harrison), 32–34
Reminiscences of Peace and War (Pryor), 104–5
Richmond, Virginia, 61–63, 99–105, 163–64
Richmond Examiner, 96–98
Richmond Sentinel, 102–3
"Robert Small" (Brown), 79–83
Robinson, Irene, 194
Rockingham Register (VA), 116–18
Ruffin, Edmund, xi, xii, 13–15, 206–7

The Sack and Disruption of the City of Columbia, S.C. (Simms), 191–93
Saxton, Rufus, 66–67
Scott, Winfield, 22–25
secession, 3–5, 10, 13, 26–28
Seddon, James, 105, 142–44, 188–89
sermons, 29–31, 73–75
Shepperson, William, 76–78

Sherman, William T., 145–46, 191

Simms, William Gilmore, 191–93

Sketches of the Rise, Progress, and Decline of Secession (Brownlow), 56–58

slave narratives and accounts: Farmer, 199–201; Grandy, 49–50; Hughes, 165–66, 173–77; Jackson, 40–41; Jones, 20–21; Maxwell, 194–96; Washington, 202–5; Webb, 6–9

slavery: at center stage in Civil War, xiv; death of slave woman, 113–15; emancipation, xii, 185–90, 194–96, 199–201; escapes and runaway, 22–25, 76–78, 116–18, 163–64; "faithful" slave Nathan, article on, 86–87; fear of rebellions, 16–19, 183–84; impressment, 142–44; Lenoir on, 135–37; Mammy figure, 76–78, 104; masters and slaves in occupied Mississippi, 126–27; secession and, 4; Stephens's "Cornerstone" speech, 10–12; transition to free labor, 171–72. *See also* African Americans

Smalls, Robert, 79–83

Sorrel, Moxley, 33

1st South Carolina Volunteers, 197–98

"A Southern Scene from Life" (Shepperson), 76–78

"Speech at Columbia" (Davis), 178–79

Splitler, J. Wayne, 117–18

Stephens, Alexander, 10–12

Stewart, Robert, 64–65

Stone, Kate, 53–55, 106–10

The Story of Mattie J. Jackson (Jackson), 40–41

Strong, George C., 84–85

Stuart, Addy, 93–95

Stuart, Jeb, xv

Taylor, Samuel S., 199

Thirty Years a Slave (Hughes), 165–66, 173–77

Tillson, William H., 140–41

Twain, Mark, 35–39

Up From Slavery (Washington), 202–5

Vicksburg, Battle of, 131, 163, 183

Waddell, Joseph Addison, 93–95

Wallace, Lewis "Lew," 8–9

War Department, Confederate, 64, 100–101, 142–44

War Department, Union, 88

Warwick, Clarence, 62

Washington, Booker T., 202–5

Watkins, Samuel R., 159–62

Webb, William, 6–9

Williamson, James Joseph, 119–20

Winder, John Henry, 102, 105

Wolf, Jacob, 118

"woman order," New Orleans, 84–85

women's diaries and memoirs: Bond, 147; Clay-Clopton, 124–25; Harrison, 32–34; Holmes, 113–15; McGuire, 61–63, 151–52; Pryor, 104–5; Stone, 53–55, 106–10. *See also* slave narratives and accounts

Works Progress Administration, 49, 194, 199